complete

bathroom

BOOK

LOWE'S
Home Improvement Warehouse

welcome home

HIGH ON THE WISH LIST FOR MANY HOMEOWNERS IS A BATHROOM REMODEL—
to spruce up a powder room for when company comes, or to improve a children's bath,
or to indulge themselves with a luxurious master bath. Whether you're thinking about
an extensive project or planning a makeover on a budget, there's a world of possibilities:
fixtures, flooring, and countertop choices; lighting, mirrors, skylights, and window
options; paint, wallpaper, and decorative touches that can complement any style, from
country farmhouse to downtown brownstone.

This book is designed to guide you through those choices to a bath that's efficient,
stylish—and just what you wanted.

Lowe's books—**Complete Home Improvement**, **Complete Landscaping**, **Complete Home
Decorating**, **Complete Kitchen**, and now **Complete Bathroom**—are part of our commit-
ment to providing everything you need for projects around your home, from great ideas,
advice, techniques, and tips to all your tools, materials, fixtures, and finishes.

Even a small bathroom remodel can be a complex undertaking. It may involve
plumbing and electrical work or tub and tile installation—even learning about building
codes and inspections. Lowe's Plumbing Sales Specialists are ready to advise you on
planning as well as tools, materials, and fixtures, and Lowe's Installed Sales Coordinators
will be happy to arrange for installers and contractors to ensure a successful outcome.
If you're going to undertake the work—or even part of it—on your own, our in-store
classes, or the wealth of information in our How-To Library on www.lowes.com, can
give you valuable guidance to tackle your project with confidence.

Lowe's has been helping people create beautiful homes for more than five decades,
so we're more than ready to work with you on your next project. For the ultimate in
beauty—and function—for your bath, come to Lowe's today.

Lowe's Companies, Inc.

Bob Tillman
CHAIRMAN/CEO/PRESIDENT

Melissa S. Birdsong
DIRECTOR, TREND
FORECASTING & DESIGN

Robin Gelly
MERCHANDISER

Bob Gfeller
SENIOR VP, MARKETING

Jean Melton
VP, MERCHANDISING

Mike Menser
SENIOR VP, GENERAL
MERCHANDISE MANAGER

Dale Pond
EXECUTIVE VP, MERCHANDISING

Ann Serafin
MERCHANDISE MANAGER

table of contents

Lowe's Series

PROJECT DIRECTOR René Klein

SENIOR EDITOR Sally W. Smith

Staff for Lowe's Complete Bathroom Book

EDITOR Don Vandervort, Hometips

MANAGING EDITOR Louise Damberg

ART DIRECTOR Dan Nadeau

TEXT & RESEARCH Carol A. Crotta, Patricia Freeman,
Rick Peters, Shelley Ring Diamond, Gabe Vandervort

ILLUSTRATION Bill Oetinger

PRODUCTION COORDINATOR Eligio Hernandez

PROOFREADER Lorna Corpus Sullivan

INDEXER Rick Hurd

PRODUCTION DIRECTOR Lori Day

DIGITAL PRODUCTION Jennifer McMillan/Color Control,
Jeff Curtis/Leisure Arts

On the cover

TOP LEFT: Photography: David Duncan Livingston.

TOP RIGHT: Photography: Jamie Hadley. Design: Brad Polvorosa.

MIDDLE: Photography: Jennifer Jordan.

BOTTOM LEFT: Photography: Mark Samu, courtesy Hearst Magazines.

BOTTOM RIGHT: Photography: Philip Harvey. Design: J. Reed Robins.

COVER DESIGN Vasken Guiragossian

10 9 8 7 6 5 4 3 2 1

First printing February 2003

Copyright © 2003

Sunset Publishing Corporation, Menlo Park, CA 94025.

First edition. All rights reserved, including the right of reproduction
in whole or in part in any form.

ISBN 0-376-00915-2

Library of Congress Control Number: 2002116663

Printed in the United States.

how to use this book

IF YOU ARE SERIOUS ENOUGH ABOUT updating, remodeling, or building a new bathroom to have picked up this book, you probably already have some sense of the task ahead. As with most things worth working for, there is sometimes a long and winding road between the idea and the execution—in remodeling, a road that travels between the peaks of dreams and the rocky terrain of financial realities. This book will provide signposts to help you reach your goal.

Whether you are looking for design ideas, help sorting through available bath-related products, advice on dealing with planning and construction, or do-it-yourself step-by-step instructions for common bathroom remodeling projects, you've come to the right guide. Here's a brief look at what lies ahead:

your **ideal** bathroom

Turn to this section for ideas, inspiration, and a real visual treat. This photo gallery starts with the big picture—how to determine your needs and end up with the right bathroom. It moves on to a visual survey of today's specialized bathrooms, from master baths to powder rooms, children's baths, and shared bathrooms. It illuminates the range of design possibilities, from simple makeovers to major remodels, demonstrates clever ways to think about space and to bring the outdoors in, and presents effective bathroom layouts. Finally, it spotlights universal and accessible design, bathroom storage options, and functional and decorative details that can make an ordinary bathroom extraordinary.

buyer's guide

This indispensable, concise guide to the array of bathroom-related products currently on the market will aid you in making the right choices for your needs. Bathroom elements considered here encompass bathtubs and showers, including spa whirlpool tubs, tub-shower combinations, prefabricated units, and all types of enclosures; showerheads and shower and tub faucets; toilets and bidets; sinks and their faucets; countertops; bathroom storage options; hardware and fittings; flooring options; paint and wallcoverings; lighting and ventilation; doors, windows, and skylights; and window treatments.

A gallery of stunning, idea-filled bathrooms will guide you through every step of planning and designing your ideal bathroom.

Each project presented in the Do-It-Yourself Guide offers illustrated step-by-step instructions.

project **workbook**

Once you have made the decision to remodel your bathroom, you will face a number of important considerations as you develop your plan. This section takes you through the development phase, including a helpful planning questionnaire; discussions about creating a budget, financing the project, and dealing with the unexpected; hiring and managing professionals; utilizing Lowe's installation services; handling plans and contracts; working with codes, permits, and zoning; managing your project; and giving attention to bathroom safety issues.

do-it-yourself **guide**

If you count yourself among the handy and would like to do some, or most, of the remodeling work yourself, this section offers a series of well-illustrated step-by-step instructions for accomplishing the most common bathroom remodeling projects. These include opening up walls and building a simple wall, hanging and finishing drywall, and installing interior trim; plumbing tasks such as installing faucets, toilets, and several different kinds of sinks; electrical improvements, including wiring receptacles and switches, and installing vanity lights and light/fan fixtures; and installing a variety of flooring materials, countertops, cabinetry, medicine cabinets, and accessories. To help get you started, we have included a guide to the tools and materials you'll use to complete the projects.

Throughout the book, you will be treated to easy-to-read graphic presentations, as demonstrated on these pages. In addition to the clear step-by-step instructions, there are cautionary safety messages for do-it-yourselfers. Floor plans are presented where helpful. And Lowe's Quick Tips, located in the margins, are loaded with professional advice for streamlining the job.

LOWE'S QUICK TIP

Tip boxes in the margins offer helpful ideas and time-saving advice.

a special retreat

IT IS, PERHAPS, A HALLMARK OF OUR TIMES THAT THE POPULARITY OF BATH-
rooms has skyrocketed. Not so long ago, it wasn't unusual to find a two- or three-
bedroom house serviced by a single full bath and a half bath, or powder room, for
guests. The bathrooms themselves were generally modest affairs, 5 feet by 7 feet
being the standard size, and rarely scenes of extravagance.

Today, all that is changing. At least part of this trend is due to real estate pricing—
the more bathrooms, the higher a house's asking price. But there
also seems to be a deeper need at work here. We want more baths,
and we want better baths, because we increasingly are looking to
the bathroom for something beyond simple hygiene. We want a
retreat from whatever the world outside and inside the home may
be dishing out. We want private spaces where we can relax, pam-
per ourselves, and emerge refreshed and rejuvenated. We want
bathrooms that are well designed and look updated and stylish.
And we are willing to pay more for them.

The good news is that the bath industry and bath designers
have found ingenious ways to provide all, or at least some, of the
amenities of the modern spa at affordable prices for even the hum-
blest bathrooms in the most modest homes. Specialized showerheads; whirlpool baths in all sizes; inspired turns on traditional
tub, sink, and fixture designs; improved heating and ventilation systems; sophisticated
lighting systems; eye-catching new surface materials—such innovations have let us
view the bathroom with appreciative new eyes.

You may be embarking on a major bath remodel in the quest for the perfect home
spa, or you simply may be looking to bring out the best in your 5-by-7. In the end, a
well-appointed bath is more than just an asset, it is a true pleasure.

your ideal bathroom

IF YOU WERE PICKING UP THIS BOOK ONLY A GENERATION AGO, YOUR CONCEPT of the ideal bathroom would probably be very straightforward. You'd imagine a small room tucked between bedrooms, equipped with a sink, mirror, toilet, and tub-and-shower combination. It would be neat, discreet, and designed to perform efficiently.

What a difference a few decades make. Our current image of the ideal bath has less in common with the American notion of the last century than it does with that of the ancient Romans. Like the Romans, who traveled the world to construct luxurious thermae around natural hot springs, we look to the bathroom more as a place of rest, relaxation, and rejuvenation—a private retreat from the rigors of life.

Of course, not everyone has the space or the means to create an elaborate spa bathroom, but technological advances by a host of manufacturers make it possible for nearly everyone to enjoy some of the same benefits in more-modest bathrooms.

In the following pages, you will take a photo-rich guided tour through the world of baths and bathroom remodeling, from powder rooms and children's baths to knock-your-socks-off master baths. You will learn about making changes that are true to the style of your home—including the functional and decorative details that

The steamy Roman public baths in Bath, England, are as enticing today as they were 2,000 years ago.

make all the difference—using space to great advantage, and bringing the outdoors in. There are practical chapters on the best bath layouts, storage solutions, outfitting a bath for the physically challenged, and making the most of a shared bathroom. And to illustrate the impressive difference your efforts can make, we show you before and after photos of both major remodels and simple makeovers.

Our intent is to inspire and inform you, and set you firmly on the road to creating your own ideal bathroom.

Setting the right mood means getting all the details right—here, an elegant Greek key tile mosaic, coordinating shower curtain, and antique-style shower set blend seamlessly.

getting it right

WHEN PLANNING A NEW BATHROOM, it's very helpful to have a clear goal. For most of us, the main goal is to create a great bathroom. Of course, "great" is a relative term. But there's general agreement that successful bathrooms work on several levels. Great bathrooms look stun-

A colorful mix of woods, burnished walls, and no-frills mirror perfectly harmonize in this warm contemporary bathroom.

ning as a result of wonderful choices of finishes and fixtures. They often have plenty of natural light and may even capture a view. And they are comfortable—if not downright luxurious—to use.

Of course, the elements that make a particular bathroom design successful depend upon its intended use. A powder room, or half bath, where guests can quickly freshen up is often a dramatic setting. A well-designed children's bath is usually a colorful, fun, and functional environment. A shared bath needs to gracefully accommodate more than one family member or guest while complementing the bedrooms it serves. And the master bath, generally the largest bathroom of all, is designed to be an adult oasis of relaxation.

Most important, all bathrooms should function well. To that end, don't scrimp on fixtures. Buy a quality toilet that utilizes water-saving technology; a well-made sink; and a solid tub, shower, or tub-shower combination. Key bathroom fixtures are an important investment that will repay you over time with trouble-free use. If you must cut corners, buy less-expensive surface materials or cabinetry—you'll be more likely to want to change these at some point anyway.

Before you start the design process, answer two important questions: Who will use this bath, and what will make it a great bath for that individual or individuals? Your answers will help you prioritize features and distill your ideas. For exam-

This understated traditional bathroom is elevated by clever touches, such as the comfortable built-in storage bench in the dressing area and mirror-mounted light.

ple, you might discover you want to install a spacious shower stall instead of a tub-shower combination in your teenage son's bathroom, since many boys rarely use a tub. For an athlete, consider a shower with spa-style jet sprays to pound out weary muscles. On the other hand, a tub-shower combination might be a better choice for a couple. For someone who has long hair (or who bathes the dog in the shower), a flexible hand-held showerhead for hair washing can be a boon.

Similarly, children's bathrooms call for safety features such as anti-scald valves;

and a bathroom that works for anybody should be equipped with stainless-steel grab bars in the tub area and alongside the toilet. In both cases, consideration should be given to using materials that are resilient and nonskid. You can save the marble or granite to make an elegant design statement in the powder room.

When designing your new bathroom, be clear about how the room will be used, pay attention to the needs and requirements of those who will use it, and choose high-quality materials that look stunning. Your result will be a great bathroom.

getting it right

LEFT: Getting it right need not involve great expense. Here, inexpensive tiles, both large and small, in cream, beige, and white mix beautifully with the simple pedestal sink and oversized mirror. BELOW: The tub's elegance is emphasized and complemented by the formal pattern of the wall niches.

This perfectly coordinated bathroom is distinguished by a classical suite of brass fittings—including window hardware—plus crown molding, window and mirror frames, and tub surround to match the cabinetry.

Like most master baths, this stylish example aims to make a sophisticated statement, with skylight-pierced high ceilings, broad windows, elegant lighting, and beautiful materials.

巧
天
雲
造
小
不
思
另

master baths

THE MASTER BATH IS THE PREMIER bathroom in the house—and yet it is a relative newcomer to the world of baths. The idea of a bathroom devoted solely to the adult inhabitants of the house is not new, of course, but a master bathroom remodel has become one of the improvements most desired by homeowners.

In its simplest form, the master bath typically is outfitted with a shower and/or tub, dual sinks, and a toilet. But these elements are only a fraction of the story for many of today's master baths. In recent years, the master bath has evolved to encompass the features of the master suite, including a sitting room, dressing area, and—in some cases—even an exercise room or entertainment center.

This new master suite is essentially an adult retreat—indeed, it is sometimes described in terms usually reserved for fine resorts: "an oasis of calm," or "a peaceful refuge." In reality, today's master baths are designed to be true home spas, a yin-and-yang combination of relaxation and stimulation.

The separate tub, for example, is not simply a tub but comes equipped with whirlpool jets and more. Often it is elevated and surrounded by windows, affording a view of the outdoors. Water cascades into these large tubs from wide-mouthed waterfall faucets. A newer style of tub is actually a soaking-tub-within-a-tub featuring water, illuminated in a timed sequence of soothing colors, that gently cascades over the edges. Spending time in a bath like this is an event.

Showers, of course, aren't simply showers but, as one manufacturer calls them, "shower destinations." They feature multinozzled, adjustable, and temperature-controlled water-jet systems designed to pound away the stress from muscles you

The dual-sink vanity is standard for a master bath, as are separated tub and shower areas.

didn't even know you had. There are steam showers as well, designed to replicate the soothing steam-bath experience. Add to this mix a cozy dressing area with overstuffed couches, a good sound system, adjustable mood lighting, and perhaps even an espresso station, and it becomes hard to imagine how anyone makes it out the door to carry on with the day's work.

The most elaborate master baths demand a significant amount of space, much more than simply knocking out a closet or annexing a small bedroom. Moreover, they can be tricky remodels, depending on the age of the house—the

A spacious shower is paired with a raised whirlpool tub designed for rest and relaxation.

vastly increased water weight borne by these large tubs can literally send them crashing through an inadequately supported older floor. The house may need serious reinforcing by reliable contractors. For that reason, remodels incorporating master bath spas tend to be in single-story houses or second-story additions.

If neither of those situations is yours, take heart. Today's technology has introduced high-grade specialty nozzles that can be retrofitted into most standard showerheads, and lightweight whirlpool tubs of varying sizes that work in less-than-gargantuan bathrooms.

Above all, the master bath is a matter of attitude. If you work to make it a retreat, by creating the right atmosphere through paint and/or wallpaper, attractive fixtures of good quality, elegant flooring and countertop materials, a dimmer switch for the lights, and perhaps even a candle or two, your own spa will be open for business.

ABOVE: Separate-but-equal grooming stations ease the way for two adults to get ready at the same time. LEFT: A two-way fireplace set in the wall between master bedroom and bathroom is the ultimate luxury.

Piercing an exterior wall with a series of gracefully etched and arched glass panels lets light in spectacularly.

the masterful bath In the master-bath-as-spa, no element is more important than the bathtub, which very often is set in a niche to serve as the room's focal point. Today's tubs are larger than ever, often built for two as a romantic, relaxing, and rejuvenating way to pass the evening. These oversize tubs are perfect for good, long soaking, and many also come equipped with high-tech jets to pulse tired bodies into blissful oblivion.

powder rooms

THOUGH THE VERY NOTION OF A "powder room"—a place to which the ladies retire to take the shine off their noses—is charmingly dated, today's powder room is anything but. There is simply no substitute for this indispensable small bathroom, also called a half bath. The primary components—sink, mirror, and toilet—are a given, but it's in the handling of these basic elements that the

powder room blossoms. When done right, powder rooms can be little jewels.

The first consideration for a powder room is its location. If you are starting from scratch, the most successful placement is likely to be off a hallway, for privacy. It should not open to any public rooms. If you are remodeling an existing powder room, and its location is problematic, you may be better off reconfiguring access to the room, or turning it into a closet and searching out a more suitably situated spot.

Because the quarters are usually quite tight, powder rooms can be tricky. In many cases, it takes a bit of imaginative problem-solving to keep the room from feeling cramped.

All bathrooms benefit from having a window, but many powder rooms have none. In this situation, it's important—in fact, it may be required by local codes—to install a good ventilation system. Excellent lighting also helps. Soft, flattering, indirect lighting works best, particularly since the close proximity of highly reflective surfaces will exaggerate any glare. If you really want to make your guests feel good, use a beauty salon tip and install pale-pink light bulbs, which lend a rosy, healthy glow to any complexion.

Because there's so little furniture in a powder room, you can go dramatic with impunity. Indulge in a sculptural sink that becomes a piece of functional art. Interesting sinks abound today, ranging from glass, metal, and even concrete to

A quaint wicker grooming table and chair set adds a graceful finishing touch to a powder room decorated with floral patterns.

Mission meets modern in this simple bathroom, with cleverly plumbed basin and table evoking a simpler time.

An angled mirror
bounces window light
into this small space,
while an illuminated shelf
adds visual interest.

artfully painted ceramic. An increasingly popular look, particularly if there is some space, is the decorative sink set in an ornate chest or other piece of actual furniture—you can have such a piece cut and plumbed to receive a sink.

There are faucet sets, from elaborate to ultrasleek, in proportions that are perfect for the small powder room. The mirror should be large and well lit—remember the powder room's original purpose. For

the walls, intense colors can be surprisingly effective, but keep the ceiling lighter in a truly small space. Of all the rooms in the house, this one is perfect for *trompe l'oeil* or other decorative painting, especially if there is no window.

With the great variety of powder room appointments available today—including clever corner or compact sinks and toilets—you can turn even the smallest space into a gem of a powder room.

LEFT: Dark tones and golden light add depth and mystery to this romantic rendition. BELOW: A corner sink's curving lines streamline the small space, while the built-in mirror reflects natural light into the room.

Dramatically carved curves—in the mirror and cabinet—give a sculptural touch to this powder room.

children's baths

IF YOUR HOME HAS A BATHROOM USED almost entirely by children, why not tailor it to suit their needs and preferences? A child's bathroom can be designed with features that make the space safer, more comfortable, and—with lively decor and amenities—more fun to use than a bathroom designed with adults in mind.

Most of the elements that make children's bathrooms right for kids are easy to change or modify as the children grow— or they are features that work for everyone. Though a low sink cabinet in a five-year-old's bathroom might make

brushing teeth far easier at this age, it would soon be outgrown. Instead, a hideaway stepstool is a better, more temporary solution for boosting the child's reach to the sink. Pull-out sink faucets and shower nozzles make hair washing and general bathing more fun than trauma.

Designing a child-friendly bathroom is, above all, about safety—and safety starts with the basic materials. Use slip-resistant flooring such as vinyl tile or, at the very least, heavily textured ceramic tile. If you use rugs, be sure they're skidproof. When purchasing a new tub, buy one with a fully textured bottom. If you are not changing the tub and it has a smooth bottom, you can purchase colorful textured stick-on appliqués, or an extralong textured shower mat. A stainless-steel grab bar, set at a child's height above the tub edge, gives an extra measure of protection against slips. A shower curtain is a better option than glass doors for a child's bath because it allows you easier access for

Celebrate a child's bath by indulging in color. BELOW: Bright red details are a bold stroke in this teen bathroom. RIGHT: The sun-and-sea paint treatment highlights the playful tile border.

helping; if you do opt for a sliding-door tub enclosure, it should be shatterproof and impact-resistant. Scald-prevention or pressure-balancing valves make the bathroom more user-friendly for everyone.

Of course, a child's bathroom can be every bit as whimsical, colorful, and imaginatively designed as the bedroom. When children see the bath as a bright and happy place, hygiene becomes play instead of a chore. Happily, manufacturers have created materials aimed solely at children's baths. Tile, for example, is available in a wide palette of lively colors and motifs.

Depending on their ages, you may want to involve your kids in the design process. It helps to come up with a theme—nautical, jungle, garden, for example—or else just a basic color scheme. Winnow down the materials selections to an acceptable handful (unless you really would like a black-and-slime-green bathroom) and let the kids have a say. They will feel proud to have created their own environment, and it will be a memorable experience for all.

Making good use of otherwise wasted space, high-set cabinets are also safe storage solutions for supplies.

Tucking the tub and toilet
behind a frosted-glass
pocket door creates
privacy zones within
a shared bathroom.

shared baths

SHARED BATHS—THOSE SERVING MORE than one person, or perhaps the entire family—can sometimes be scenes of not-so-quiet chaos. Toiletries and towels fight for space in too-small cabinets, and a single sink and mirror often becomes the site of daily skirmishes.

If such is the scene in your household, take heart: Remodeling a shared bathroom offers the opportunity to make that bath do double, triple, or even quadruple duty efficiently and with style.

To be sure, it can be a challenge. The very notion of a shared bath treads heavily on one of the bathroom's greatest pleasures—privacy. The key to successful remodeling of a shared bath is to allow every user to enjoy some personal space. To do that effectively, think in terms of multiples as you plan your remodel.

One of the best and easiest solutions is to install two sinks, either separate pedestals, each with its own mirror, or a single vanity with two sinks served by one large mirror. Two pedestals create two completely separate grooming stations (although for plumbing purposes it is best to locate them along the same wall). Dual-sink vanities provide a less cluttered look and more counter space and storage, generally preferable for a smaller bathroom. Whichever option you choose, make sure each station has adequate lighting, preferably on its own switch, and its own electrical outlet to accommodate simultaneous tasks such as hair drying and shaving.

The next consideration for a shared bath is creating private storage space. Every user should have at least a couple of shelves to call his or her own for personal hygiene products. If you choose to install a dual-sink vanity, you will want one that has at least two cupboards and several drawers. Similarly, if you put in separate pedestals, install separate storage cabinetry adjacent to each, plus medicine cabinets behind the mirrors. Separate

This bathroom employs glass-brick walls and swinging doors with obscured glass to establish private areas within the space.

towel racks also make sharing a bath easier and neater, reducing the likelihood of a wet-towel pileup.

If a bath is shared by two people who don't mind using it at the same time, you can consider a few more options, such as an extra-large, dual-head shower stall. The showerheads, which can be installed on the same wall or on opposite walls, should have individual controls. A toilet can be tucked behind a low wall or even behind a decorative screen.

If sharing a bathroom at the same time is more an undesirable necessity, you can enhance a shower's privacy by making sure all walls and the shower door are opaque; it will probably benefit from a waterproof shower light. Similarly, a bathtub can be cloaked by a freestanding screen, a translucent pocket door, or even a ceiling-mounted curtain that can be drawn around the tub. Conceal the toilet in the classic "water closet" behind a full or pocket door.

The challenges presented by a shared bathroom are met by providing dual sinks, mirrors, and storage accessories.

shared baths

LEFT: **This brilliant customized solution to a shared sink is an extra-long oval with diagonally set taps at either end, and separate towel racks.** BELOW: **If you have the room, back-to-back vanities can create a grooming "island" with separate stations.**

Providing sinks and storage for two can crowd a room, but clean-lined built-in cabinets and discreet lighting make this bathroom sleekly efficient.

what's your style?

HAVE YOU GIVEN MUCH THOUGHT TO the overall style of your new bathroom? During a remodel, particularly if you're changing many or most of the fixtures and surfaces in the room, you have the opportunity to make choices of colors, materials, and decorative motifs that evoke any of many decorating styles. Doing this can help personalize the room and give its design focus.

Decorating styles have characteristics that identify them with a particular region, era, or artistic movement. Choosing one for a bathroom isn't difficult. If your house boasts a pronounced architectural style—Victorian, contemporary, Arts and Crafts, or Mediterranean, for example—you can start with elements of that vernacular. Most major bathroom-product manufacturers feature lines that suit several of these styles, including modern versions of period looks, for everything from faucets to lighting. Magazines devoted to period restorations also carry advertisements from specialty purveyors who can deliver salvaged and rehabilitated originals. And, of course, there's the Internet marketplace, where you can find just about anything.

Those who live in an ultramodern house might opt for sleek metal and glass sinks serviced by sinuous faucets, futuristic shower systems, a squared-off tub, and tinted glass and metallic tiles for a stunning visual impact. A Victorian bath might be outfitted with small black-and-white hexagonal tile flooring, pedestal sink, wall-

mounted soap dish and cup holder, claw-foot tub with wraparound shower-curtain rod, and a high-backed toilet with pull flush. Indulging in a period look can be fun, and the range of new products in all styles means you won't have to forgo any of today's technologies.

If, as is the case for many of us, your home has no distinct architectural style, you can easily find design inspiration for your bathroom remodel in any number of places. Baths attached to bedrooms may simply be done in the colors and style of the bedroom. For a shared bath, you might choose a color that's energizing or soothing, depending on the desires of the

ABOVE: **Sleek black and white materials give a decidedly modern and masculine ambience to this bathroom.** RIGHT: **Claw-foot tub and old-fashioned fixtures impart a turn-of-the-century feeling.**

A single color may be
all good design requires,
as this glistening all-
white bath demonstrates.

individuals who use it, and coordinate the elements from there. A particular tile, a style of cabinetry, a beautiful sink or faucet you've fallen in love with—these can be good springboards to an overall design scheme. Anything can be the hook to a comprehensive design; you just have to be consistent once you have chosen a style or motif.

Of course, you don't have to do a complete remodel to communicate style. Simple things can make a big difference. Watch for a knockout set of towels. Consider replacing all of the fixtures with one fixture "suite" that includes coordinating sink and tub faucets and handles, showerhead, towel racks, toilet paper holder, perhaps even soap dishes, and cup and toothbrush holders. A few minor elements can create a dynamic overall look.

The floral motif, soft drapery, and upholstered furnishings make this classic bathroom a feminine place to rest and refresh.

Dark wood wainscoting and deep-green walls are pleasantly balanced by the brightness of the wall-mounted corner sink, the toilet, and white towels.

Country-style charm is evoked by an old-fashioned tub in an arched alcove, beadboard wainscot, and a painted chest.

RIGHT: **Sleek and sensual describes this contemporary bath, which boasts a sculpted curved-sink basin.**

BELOW: **This faux-granite composite tub appears to be a modern interpretation of the ancient Roman bath.**

RIGHT: **Deep sill, wraparound open shelving, and superimposed mirror are stylish solutions to a tight space.**

bold is beautiful A standard vanity and sink area takes on new luster when decked out in traditional details, such as the multitone counter and backsplash tiling, formal two-tone wallpaper, delicate sconces, and whimsical bird-on-a-branch mirror. The green-and-gold color theme is complemented by the dotted-swiss shower curtain and set off by the vibrant blue tile flooring.

simple makeovers

IF A MAJOR REMODEL IS NOT IN YOUR budget, you can still have the pleasures of a rejuvenated bath. You'll be amazed at what an eye-opening difference you can make without breaking the bank. Start by assessing your bath's strengths and weaknesses, and consider some of the following economical ways to perk it up.

PAINT It's been said over and over because it's true: Paint is the least expensive, yet most versatile, remodeler's tool. Giving a bath a new coat of paint, perhaps combining paint with wallpaper along the sink wall or a border trim along the ceiling junction, can do wonders. Consider painting a colorful mural along one wall, or using one of the many interesting paint techniques such as sponging or stenciling to give walls added texture and depth. Since mildew is a potential problem in most baths, make sure to stir in a fungicide additive before applying the paint.

LIGHTING Nothing makes quite as much difference to the appearance and functionality of a bathroom as good light, yet many older baths suffer from inadequate lighting. Replace worn-out or low-voltage sconces flanking the sink with new, more powerful lights or multibulb light strips. If you only have an overhead light, consider installing a mirror the size of the vanity over the sink to reflect the light and visually enlarge the room without the bother and expense of installing new electrical outlets.

NEW FIXTURES Old corroded fixtures can really date a bathroom. On the other hand, new fixtures give a polished look to a bathroom. Be sure to replace all of the fixtures—sink, tub, and shower—at the same time, with the same style "suite." Buy the best you can afford, preferably solid brass fixtures, which have long life.

REFACING CABINETS If you have a very large vanity or several cabinets in your bathroom, it might be more economical to reface rather than replace them.

The differences in this small bathroom makeover are in the details: smartly angled sink, chic black-and-white-tile motif, updated casement window, elegant sconces, and a new low wall separating tub and toilet.

Refacing cabinets with new doors is an easy, relatively inexpensive process and gives the bath a whole new look. Or, if your cabinets aren't too damaged, you can simply paint them.

REGLAZING THE TUB Replacing a chipped or rusted tub is one of the costlier remodeling jobs since it usually requires breaking into a wall. You can buy about five years' time on your tub if you have it reglazed, a process that, if done properly by a reputable company, will chemically bond a simulated porcelain finish onto it.

DECORATIVE DETAILS For an incredibly quick and easy facelift, replace cabinet knobs, pulls, and hinges. Choose new towel racks and a toilet-paper holder in the same style as the sink, shower, and tub fixtures. Cover cracked tile flooring with luxurious soft-pile scatter rugs. Finally, coordinate the rugs to make your budget bathroom a real beauty.

decorative update Rejuvenating an old bathroom can be as simple as a paint job, especially if it's done as charmingly as here. Cream and yellow horizontal striping creates a sunny atmosphere complemented nicely by the freshly painted cabinetry. New fixtures, a stylish roman shade, and stackable wicker-basket storage offer big effect at a modest cost.

LEFT: An inexpensive reed shade and framed mirror contribute to the masculine mood set by mosaic-detailed floor and wainscoting.

ABOVE: A rich paint treatment on walls, simple wallpaper border, and a fanciful curtain and hamper are simple ways to distinguish a small bathroom.

RIGHT: The theme is curves—in the vanity, mirror, tub, and shower-curtain ring—which adds dimension and personal style to an otherwise ordinary bathroom.

major remodels

IF YOU'RE PLANNING A MAJOR REMODEL or building an addition from scratch, you have the opportunity to achieve the bathroom of your dreams—budget permitting, of course. Major remodels often involve going down to the subfloor for new set-in flooring and into the wall studs for tub and shower, piercing the ceiling and roof for skylights and exterior walls for windows, and breaking through interior walls to annex more space from adjacent closets or rooms.

Be aware that a bathroom, even a small one, is one of the most complex rooms of the house, involving, for instance, both plumbing and electrical installation. In

Smart design choices— hiding a washer-dryer behind a bifold door, using antique furnishings and an extra-long shower curtain—helped turn this ungainly 6-by-20-by-10-foot room into a comfortable and multi-functional bathroom.

This wood-trimmed bathroom is only 7 by 10 feet, but positively inspired by a clever design: A room-wide shower with two doors flanks the metal sink set on a custom-made wood pedestal cabinet. When unlit, the shower fades from view, creating a cozier powder-room ambience.

addition, taking the room down to the studs is akin to building an entirely new space, with all that implies—permits, building codes, and inspections. Lowe's Plumbing Sales Specialist and professional installers can be a big help when taking on this kind of task. Or you can seek the help of an outside independent designer or contractor. Be sure to read through the Project Workbook that begins on page 134 so you will understand everything your remodel entails.

major remodels

Of course, one way to keep costs in check is to take on all or part of the work yourself. If you do this, be extremely realistic about your skills. Missteps in tiling a tub area or waterproofing a shower could cause serious water damage to your home. Most bathroom materials are pricey, so poor workmanship can be costly. At the very least, you may want to use professionals for the most demanding or complicated tasks, leaving for yourself the finish work, such as cabinet installation and painting.

You can also trim the cost of a major remodel by modifying your plans or making some compromises before the plaster starts to fly. If at all possible, work within the existing footprint of the house. Adding on to a structure almost always involves pouring a new foundation, building exterior walls, and extending the roof—all of which are expensive jobs. Pushing a bathroom out even a modest amount can be a prohibitively expensive way to gain just a few usable square feet.

Making use of existing plumbing lines and electrical wiring can be a huge cost saver. Though you don't want to limit the possibilities of your new bathroom unnecessarily, explore every layout option that will allow you to to make use of existing hookups.

Think creatively. Depending on your bathroom's orientation, replacing a window with a garden window, or using mirrors, shiny surface materials, and pale paint colors to reflect light, might accomplish as much as the far more expensive option of adding a skylight. Repainting or refacing cabinetry—particularly if your bathroom has a lot of it—can save you a bundle compared with completely replacing it. If you can cut back in these areas, you can spend your dollars on the elements that matter most, such as flooring, tile, and key fixtures.

A floor-to-ceiling tiled wall masks a standard-size tub; the offset opening aligns with a grid of glass block set in the outside wall to let in natural light.

ABOVE: **A standard 5-by-7-foot bathroom is tightly redesigned using a rounded sink to save space, sink-to-ceiling mirrored wall to enlarge it visually, and tile wainscoting for a clean-lined finish.** RIGHT: **Tub-area wall niches boost storage capacity.**

a sense of space

YOU MIGHT THINK THAT BATHROOMS would be easier to design than other rooms because they are generally smaller. On the contrary, a compact space quickly feels claustrophobic or cluttered without careful planning. In fact, even a good-sized bathroom can seem crowded when it's filled up with dual sinks, storage furni-

This elegant tub is given an equally elegant setting, framed by twin wall niches that echo the tub's shape.

ture, a bathtub, and a separate shower. Fortunately, there are a number of design tricks that can help you make the most of your bathroom.

In general, the smaller the bathroom, the more floor area you should be able to see. This may mean opting for a pedestal or wall-mounted sink in place of a vanity, and planning wall cabinets and niches for storage. It also helps to keep the sight

lines clean and simple. Curving edges—on sink, vanity, and cabinets—minimize visual obstacles and make moving around the space easier.

Many small bathrooms feature one meager light fixture centered on the ceiling, or an overhead light plus a couple of small sconces beside the mirror. But lighting, though often overlooked, can make a space feel larger when it's well conceived.

Ideally, the room's entire perimeter should be lit. And don't forget the importance of daylight; skylights can open a small space dramatically, as can generously sized windows.

Raising or vaulting the ceiling is a sure way to create a sense of volume but, if you want to avoid major construction, you can employ a number of less invasive tactics. You can reduce visual clutter by choosing paint and tile in one light color or closely related light shades. Choose tile with a small pattern or no pattern, but feel free to combine different tile textures—such as a braided backsplash trim with tile squares—for interest. Set floor tile on a diagonal to pull the eye more easily through the space. Special paint techniques can also do wonders for a small bathroom. Try painting a cloud-dotted sky above the tub or shower, or a mural vista on a wall to visually break through the room's space.

Though mirror tiles can look dated (and are not recommended in earthquake, tornado, or hurricane country), mirrors remain one of the best and most economical ways to make a small space seem

Taking advantage of the roofline's slant, this generously sized skylight provides both illumination and ventilation.

larger. Try hanging a large framed mirror on the wall opposite the sink mirror, or smaller ones flanking a vanity alcove—not only will they help you see yourself better for grooming purposes, but they will open the room visually.

Thinking about space also means creating a sense of place—setting a scene to establish a bathroom's ambience. Techniques for doing this go beyond solutions for dealing with a small bathroom. If a capacious master bath is too large and open, with no focal point, it can feel cold and uninviting. Setting the vanity area into an alcove, or creating an alcove around it, can highlight the area visually and set it apart. Positioning a beautifully appointed soaking tub on a slightly elevated platform against a bank of windows creates drama. Even something as simple as placing the tub behind a swagged ceiling-to-floor curtain can lend mystery and a touch of whimsy. Thinking creatively about how to make the most of your space will pay off with a bathroom that is truly special.

Smartly combining multiple light sources and sink-to-ceiling mirror magically enlarges this small attic bathroom.

a sense of space

ABOVE: When light meets white, the optical effect is brilliant, and visual barriers disappear.

ABOVE: A curved corner cabinet and floor-to-ceiling mirrors make the most of a small powder room area.

LEFT: A glass panel in place of a solid wall brings light to an otherwise dark shower.

RIGHT: **Twin skylights flanking a large overhead light combine to set the stage for this niched tub.**

BELOW: **This airy cove ceiling's misty blue** *trompe l'oeil* **sky visually expands the bathroom's horizons.**

ABOVE: **A skylight and decorative glass-block treatment combine to efficiently light this small, high-ceilinged bathroom.**

a winning combination Despite the small space and awkward shape, this bathroom works, thanks to its cleverly eclectic combination of efficient details. The claw-foot tub and faucet, drop shower curtain, and tile work seem to hark back to an earlier time, yet the room-ringing metal shelf, bowl sink, and sconce are decidedly modern.

the great outdoors

MAYBE IT'S A PRIMAL LONGING FOR the lost Garden of Eden, but there is something intoxicating about the sense of bathing outdoors, under sun or stars, surrounded by beautiful foliage and flowers. And though the reality of bathing out-

Glass picture windows that form a corner offer a seamless view from inside; blinds provide privacy from the outside.

doors is not very practical for most of us, bath designers, more than ever, are seeking to break down the barriers between indoors and outdoors.

Some of the more involved methods of accomplishing this new openness demand an experienced contractor and perhaps even an architect. But a moderately expe-

rienced home remodeler can tackle some of the work successfully.

Take the garden window, for example. A staple of many kitchen designs, the garden window is of glass-and-metal or -wood construction; it juts out from the wall a good foot or more, extending both usable and visual space. A garden window in the bathroom, ideally situated over the bathtub, expands the room, provides a good view of the garden beyond, and brings in a great deal of natural light—always a plus in a bathroom. (The bathroom—often moist and warm—is a great environment for many houseplants, too.) Garden windows are particularly suited to traditional or vintage-style bathrooms.

Using opaque or frosted glass or glass block is another simple and inexpensive way to flood a space with natural light yet retain privacy. For example, you might flank the mirror over the vanity area with panels of opaque glass or glass block to let natural daylight illuminate the area much like makeup lights. Glass blocks are not new, but are being used in new ways—design possibilities are many and varied with this sturdy building material. You can, for example, pierce the exterior wall horizontally with two rows of glass blocks to spray the room with a bright shaft of light. Or you might build a shower stall with the blocks to create a shower that glows serenely.

Skylights offer another means for bringing the outdoors in. Some are opaque and faceted to intensify and soften

Sturdy, extra-large casement windows maximize this home's ocean vista, visible from the tub.

the light passing through them. Clear sky-lights can be a particularly nice feature over a tub, affording a glimpse of treetops and blue sky or stars and moon as you relax. Operable skylights, when placed directly over a shower area, can help dissipate steam and bring in fresh air.

If you want to take the Garden of Eden concept seriously, you might want to literally open the bathroom to the outdoors. A spacious walk-in shower can boast watertight wood doors that swing open to a private garden area. A generous tub can sit beneath large sliding glass windows that open to a small garden, pool, or waterfall. The trick with this type of design is to offer all the benefits of open-air bathing without losing privacy and the ability to keep out the elements. Siting is everything. Side yards often are perfect choices for a nook sheltered by fencing, walls, or tall foliage. To ensure your open bath will be private, either buy mature screen plants, or start plantings the season before you plan to remodel.

ABOVE: **Glass-block walls, glass ceiling panels, and glass shower wall let light pour in from every direction.** LEFT: **A beveled tri-panel mirror echoes the shape of the large picture window—and its view.**

A Japanese-style soaking tub conducive to contemplation benefits from its unobstructed view of the peaceful garden.

a room with a view Penetrating the bathroom's solid structure is the key to bringing the outdoors in. Here, the designer has given the bather grand views of both land and sky, setting the tub into the landscape. The full-wall picture window effectively obliterates the visual boundary between indoors and out, while the supersized skylight above the tub gives a generous view of the heavens.

LEFT: **A glass-paneled door is a simple way to open up the bathroom to the garden.**

ABOVE: **This bathtub aerie features joined glass walls and a glass dome for maximum visual exposure.** LEFT: **When obscure-glass windows are open, a staggered-brick wall lets in light and air without loss of privacy.**

layouts that work

EARLY ON DURING THE PLANNING OF a bathroom remodel, you'll be faced with determining where the main fixtures and elements will be positioned. Unlike a kitchen, for which carefully studied recommendations exist about appliance placement, a bathroom has few governing rules. And, though your design choices may be limited by the room—a standard 5-by-7 bathroom, for example, won't accommodate many options—a few considerations can guide your decision making.

FOCAL POINT As a starting place for your design, decide what you would like the focal point of your bathroom to be. It may be a grand whirlpool tub, or a beautifully tiled and appointed vanity area. If possible, make the focal point the first thing seen upon entering the bathroom, and orient the remainder of the appurtenances accordingly.

PLUMBING Some of the costliest work in a bathroom remodel can involve plumbing. If budget is a concern, you will want to lay out the bath to make use of the existing pipes, drains, and vents. Shifting plumbing from one wall to another means not only running new pipes but breaking through floors and into walls as well. Similarly, locating the new bathroom on a floor directly above an old bathroom allows you to simply run pipes up the same wall, saving time and money. Or, when adding a new bathroom, placing all the plumbing along one wall can reduce plumbing costs.

NATURAL LIGHT If the bathroom has a window or windows, lay it out to take advantage of the natural light. Morning light streaming through a bathroom window is a wonderful asset. An otherwise dark shower can be gently illuminated if set across from a window—but you will want to set in opaque glass panes for privacy. Setting a vanity between windows assures soft indirect light for grooming. Place a tub below a window bank to light up the bathing area from above.

PRIVACY For some, privacy concerns are very important. Many people prefer, for example, to set the toilet in the least visible position in the bathroom, usually tucked behind the door as it opens, or

Space in this narrow, oddly shaped powder room is maximized by setting the toilet against an angled wall, easing access to the corner storage cabinet.

between the vanity and the faucet end of the tub. You can position a toilet behind a low wall separating it from a pedestal sink, which also gives you potential new storage space. Setting the tub or shower on the same wall as the door will prevent them from becoming focal points.

UNUSUAL SPACES As you can see from the photos on these pages, even the most unusually shaped spaces can function

stylishly by making use of the many new sizes and shapes of bath appliances. Consider corner tubs, showers, and sinks for small spaces, installing storage shelves on odd-shaped walls, or setting a toilet behind a louvered closet door.

When dealing with any space, make sure to set the tub perpendicular to the floor joists, and place towel and sundries storage as far from the shower and tub as possible to minimize moisture exposure.

This side-by-side shower and tub are beautifully integrated; the tub's deck flows into the generous shower enclosure to become a comfortable seat.

Setting the tub at an angle creates instant low counter and storage space, and is a guaranteed attention-grabber.

Odd and awkward spaces can result in the most interesting designs. ABOVE: The sink as butterfly, with twin trapezoid window "wings." RIGHT: An alcove tub/shower gains prominence with an intense treatment of wall tiles.

With privacy in mind,
wood-slat partitions
separate a soaking tub
from a walk-in dual-
shower stall—and set
both apart from the
rest of the bathroom.

universal design

A BATHROOM THAT WILL WORK FOR everyone calls for a design that gives extra consideration to special needs. Even if no one in your household is elderly or disabled, it's wise to plan a bathroom that can be used by anyone—you never know when a family member might break a leg or when you'll have a guest who would benefit from a bathroom designed with universal or accessible principles.

"Universal design" and "accessible design" have similar intentions but differ slightly. Universal design strives to create an environment for people of all capabilities; accessible design creates barrier-free environments specifically for the wheelchair-bound. The goal of accessible design is to foster independence.

Universal design takes into consideration both current and predicted future needs of the household. For instance, typical features include:

■ Easily accessible storage cabinets, light and electrical switches, and shower and/or tub water controls.

■ Various stainless-steel grab bars to facilitate entering and exiting the shower and bath or accessing the toilet.

This tub seat allows a person to safely sit down and ease legs over the side of the tub; the grab bar aids standing while showering.

■ A higher toilet for those who have difficulty lowering and raising themselves.

■ Graduated counter heights to accommodate someone who needs to sit to wash up and groom.

■ Enough undercounter leg space to permit grooming comfortably.

■ Wing-blade faucet handles or motion-sensing electronic faucets that run automatically when hands are placed beneath them.

Many of these features, of course, serve to make the bathroom more user-friendly for everyone.

Accessible design follows specific standards created to assure the disabled and wheelchair-bound easy access. Doorways must be at least 32 inches wide and open to a space for a wheelchair that is at least 24 inches deep by 36 inches wide. Sinks should be set at 32 inches, with ample leg room and well-insulated pipes beneath. Accessible-design toilets are higher than standard, at 18 inches, and have extension flush handles. Some newer specialty bathtubs include seats that hydraulically lift and lower a person safely into the tub. Showers feature a minimum threshold, or none, and come equipped with water-proof adjustable seats, anti-scald hand-held shower sprayers set at appropriate heights, and multiple grab bars.

Both universal and accessible design schemes always call for shatterproof materials and slip-resistant flooring. Vinyl flooring is preferred, but if you opt for ceramic tile or stone flooring, be sure it has a textured surface.

Ringing the room with a combination of open shelving and closed cabinets provides ample—and stylish—storage and display.

bathroom storage

A SHALLOW MEDICINE CABINET AND an overcrowded vanity simply won't cut it in today's busy bathrooms, especially when more than one person frequently uses the room. Storage is fundamental to keeping bathroom paraphernalia organized, easy to find, and out of view. The challenge is maximizing storage without overwhelming the typically small space with cabinetry. With thoughtful planning, you can meet this challenge.

First, figure out what needs to be stored and think about how much space each user will require. Then evaluate the available space, the room's layout, the bathroom fixtures, and how the bathroom will be used. And explore the kinds of cabinetry and other storage options you could utilize.

Look for out-of-the-way places to steal space—the wall area above towel racks and the toilet, for example, may be able to accommodate sizable cabinets. Countertop appliance garages for hair care and other grooming products can conceal clutter on long vanities, and the garages themselves can be topped with narrow cupboards for additional items. Any type of built-in seating can conceal storage beneath.

Wall niches—great for reclaiming unused space—are relatively easy to create, especially if you are opening up the walls for other work such as plumbing and wiring. A generous tiled wall niche in the tub or shower area can hold bath soaps, shampoo, razors, and the like. If you have a tub set between two parallel

walls, the wall opposite the spigot can house a set-in towel cabinet. A long narrow niche set above or to the side of a toilet might be for toilet-paper storage. A niche between the sink and the mirror can hold hand towels, tissues, or extra bars of soap.

If the room has generous floor space, consider freestanding furniture. Traditional,

Niched shelving on a little-used tub wall ensures there's well-ventilated storage for bath essentials.

bathroom storage

small-scale linen armoires are becoming a popular bathroom item; there are modern-style versions as well, and some jazzy locker-style storage cupboards for children's baths. You might also use large woven baskets for towels or even ceramic or terra-cotta planters for stashing supplies such as soaps.

Keep in mind that the more items you choose to store in a bath the better your ventilation system should be. A drawback to closed storage is the potential for moisture build-up in the cabinets, which can result in mildewed towels and soggy tissues and toilet paper.

If moisture is a chronic problem in your bathroom, improve the ventilation system (and let that exhaust fan run until all the steam from a bath or shower has cleared out completely), and consider using open shelving or storage that has louvered or ventilated doors.

TOP: **Open wicker baskets in a custom cabinet offer plenty of easily accessible storage.** ABOVE: **A shelf set below a wall-mounted sink is perfect for towels.** RIGHT: **Backed by a space-enhancing mirror, decorative shelving is set in the wall between tub and toilet.**

Who said storage had to be square? These irregularly shaped and playfully colorful cabinets provide a stylish and spacious alternative to the standard bathroom vanity.

RIGHT: **Kitchen-style appliance garages can be a simple solution to vanity-counter clutter.**
FAR RIGHT: **A pullout wire basket serves as a hidden hamper.**

functional details

SOME OF THE MOST IMPORTANT bathroom improvements you can make aren't decorative—they're functional. These details or design features elevate the level of comfort and efficiency in the bathroom. They are often the result of creative problem solving—dealing with trouble spots in a particular design or providing clever new ways of addressing familiar problems. If you bump up against obstacles during your planning, probe the possibilities with a little outside-the-box thinking and by exploring some of the accessories currently on the market.

Just what are functional details? They're easiest to understand by example. If you live in a cold climate, a nice warm bathroom might be a priority. You could install overhead heat lamps or wall fans—both of which can be effective—but one of the most efficient and seductively comfortable ways to heat the bath is with radiant-floor heating. Or you might opt for electric towel warmers, which warm the room as well as the towels—an increasingly affordable but nonetheless luxurious addition to any bath.

Some functional details are built into the bathroom during construction or remodeling improvements. A bench seat built into a shower stall makes a handy perch, while a short wall set between the toilet and sink lends privacy and may provide storage space. If you are loath to cover your windows but would like more seclusion, consider installing opaque or frosted-glass panes. In lieu of a shower curtain in a tub-shower combination, you might try a European-style swing shower door that encloses only half the tub. In a tight bathroom with a shallow sink area, you can save room around the sink simply by setting the faucet and handles at an angle. Careful placement of mirrors, perhaps even mirroring a wall, can give

This graduated wall is dual-purpose: It lends privacy to the toilet area and creates new storage possibilities.

you better sightlines for grooming while visually opening up a small space. On the indulgent end of the functional spectrum are waterproof stereo speakers for the shower or a small media system secreted behind cabinet doors.

You may not have to remodel to add functional details; some are sold as accessories that are easy to add to any bathroom. Bath gel/shampoo/conditioner dispensers attached to the shower wall eliminate the typical multibottle congestion.

A shaving mirror installed in the shower helps get two jobs done at the same time. A magnifying mirror that accordions out from the wall at the sink is a great aid when applying makeup. You also might want to attach your blow dryer to the sink wall for quick and easy access. These are only a few of the possibilities; scan the shelves at Lowe's to discover some of the accessories and details that can turn your bathroom into a more comfortable, functional area.

The mirrored shutters around this simple window serve as both grooming aids and light reflectors.

RIGHT: **This European-style hinged glass panel simply swings into position when it's shower time.**
BELOW: **Waterproof stereo speakers are guaranteed to delight music lovers and shower singers alike.**

LEFT: **Frosting a window's lower panes is an efficient and easy way to maintain both privacy and natural light.** ABOVE: **Setting the faucet handles and spigot at angles is a simple solution to a too-shallow counter.**

the multifunctional bath This two-person shower stall features showerheads set at different heights to better serve a family. The shower-wide operable skylight delivers efficiency on two levels: as a natural source of ventilation, and as a light well. The glass doors to the shower allow the light to illuminate the shower area and also pass to the rest of the bathroom.

decorative details

WITH ANY INTERIOR DESIGN, THE handful of well-chosen decorative details is often what gives a room personality. The bathroom is no exception. In fact, its relatively small and enclosed space makes it an especially effective—and affordable—showcase for imaginative decor.

The vanity becomes the bathroom's centerpiece when given a burnished paint treatment and eye-catching hardware.

Interesting countertop and flooring patterns and materials, exceptional fixtures, unusual cabinet pulls, and paint and wallpaper treatments can all contribute to establishing a unique bath environment.

If your bath is already a certain style—contemporary, traditional, or Victorian, for example—decorative details such as a sculptural glass sink, elaborate mirror, or period faucet will strengthen and enhance the look. If your bath is of no particular style, adding details can establish a look. One special touch such as a tile mural over the bathtub, a subtly striped paint treatment on the walls, or cabinet pulls shaped like toothbrushes and toothpaste tubes may be all it takes to make your bathroom distinctive.

Any facet of the bathroom can benefit from an interesting design selection. Today, a wealth of nontraditional materials is available for bathroom use. Metals, glass, stone, and even concrete are perking up the traditional bath. Still, nothing beats ceramic tile for its versatility and decorative possibilities. Whether machine-made or handmade and hand-painted, tile comes in every color, pattern, shape, texture, and finish imaginable, with prices ranging from very reasonable to breathtakingly expensive. The wonderful thing about tile is that you can, in most cases, easily combine inexpensive tile with a few pricey ones that serve as decorative details. Try punctuating standard floor tiles with inch-wide colored-glass tile squares set at the cor-

A graceful wall-mounted sink, inlaid flooring, multi-tone wall treatment, and collection of mirrors come together to great effect in this bathroom.

ners, or sending a small school of hand-painted fish tiles swimming about in a shower stall lined with a sea of inexpensive blue field tiles. You get the idea.

Paint treatments are another fun, and often low-cost, decorative detail. Experiment with complementary colors on opposing walls; sponging, ragging, or combining other colors over a base coat; or stenciling a design to give the walls panache. A painted mural, especially of a sublime vista, is not only a nice touch in itself but a great way to open up a tight space visually. You also might combine paint or a paint treatment with a decorative wallpaper border, or wallpaper any-

thing from a single wall to the entire bathroom, ceiling included. Wallpaper designs can help set a theme, which can be carried through to the shower curtain, towels, and rugs.

Other great details are especially beautiful or unusual fixtures, such as elaborate faucets and cascade-style bath spigots for large tubs. Cabinet knobs and pulls can add style or even whimsy. As you search for interesting decorative choices for your new bathroom, be alert to those things that catch your eye and make you smile. Chances are, once they are happily installed in your bath, they will do the same for everyone who sees them.

In this new old-fashioned bath, star-shaped hardware complements the unusual curtain treatment, claw-foot tub, and free-standing spigot.

decorative details

tile style Tile is the bathroom's all-star performer in offering fascinating detail possibilities at often bargain prices. Treatments can be as simple as an inexpensive tile used in interesting color combinations, or a more expensive border tile surrounded by less expensive field tiles. Or you can open the wallet and opt for more intricate installations, such as broken-tile mosaic works, or beautifully rendered tile murals.

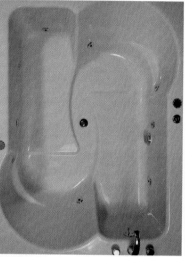

buyer's guide

SHOPPING FOR BATHROOM COMPONENTS CAN BE CHALLENGING, TO say the least. There are dozens, even hundreds, of decisions to be made. Every item, from the cabinetry to the towel bars, must be carefully selected to blend with your bathroom decor and serve your family's needs. Many products are big-ticket purchases that you'll be living with for years to come. To make matters more complicated, everything you select for the damp, confined bathroom environment must be water resistant and space efficient.

This chapter is designed to help you select products that meet the demands of your bathroom remodel. You will find an overview of the enormous array of options you'll have when outfitting your bathroom, so you can

choose the products that are right for you. Before you begin, you may want to refer back to Chapter One: Your Ideal Bathroom for some tips on creating a bath that looks and functions the way you want it to. You can also check out the Project Workbook that begins on page 134,

which will help you assess your needs and identify your priorities so you can find products with the features you want.

Once you know what you're looking for, a Lowe's Plumbing Sales Specialist can show you a wide selection of products that are perfect for your project. Lowe's also has Installed Sales Coordinators on hand to assist you with your choices, and you can arrange for installation at the same time.

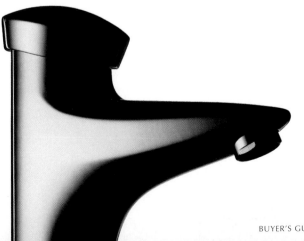

tubs & showers

TUBS AND SHOWERS TEND TO DOMI-nate a bathroom design. Their sheer size makes them conspicuous; their dimensions often determine an entire floor plan. And what fixture could loom larger when it comes to function? The tub or shower you choose can have a dramatic effect on your daily routine, not to mention your safety and comfort. Considering how much is at stake, it only makes sense to examine your options carefully.

Begin by deciding whether you want a tub, a shower, or both. This may be sole-ly a matter of preference, but sometimes it's a matter of space: The standard 5-by-7-foot family bath has room for either a shower or a tub, not one of each. When square footage is limited, a combination tub/shower is adequate for either a relax-ing soak or a quick dousing. If you're a wash-and-go bather, you may be better off using limited space for a generously proportioned stall shower, which offers easier access and firmer footing. Of course, if you're building an addition or remodeling a large bath, you can have the luxury of a tub plus the convenience of a separate shower.

This oval-shaped cast-acrylic tub churns the water with a variable-volume hydromassage system. Easy-to-clean acrylic is also light-weight, making the unit relatively easy to install.

choosing a bathtub

The National Kitchen & Bath Association categorizes bathtubs according to how they are installed. Both traditional tubs and whirlpools come in the four basic styles listed below. Within these categories, you can choose from a variety of shapes, sizes, colors, and materials. Before you buy any tub, be sure your bathroom is big enough to accommodate it. There should be a space at least 5 feet long and 30 inches wide in front of the tub so that people can climb in and out of it with ease. Many tubs are available in either right- or left-handed versions, a term that indicates which end of the tub contains a hole for the drain (it's also possible to find center-hole models, although they're less common). To determine which one you need, face the space where it will go: If the drain is on the right side, you should purchase a right-handed tub.

RECESSED TUBS The most popular type of basic bathtub is a recessed tub, also called a three-wall-alcove tub; as the name implies, it is designed to fit into an alcove or other recessed area where it can be installed against three walls. Only the front of the tub has a decorative finish; alcove walls conceal the other sides. Recessed tubs are space-efficient, affordable, and widely available. They're typi-

cally made of enameled steel, which is light and inexpensive but noisy and prone to chipping. Enameled cast iron is a more elegant, durable option if you don't mind paying a higher price and beefing up your floor to support the additional weight. The standard length for a basic tub is 60 inches, but for extra comfort you can get one that's 72 inches long. Some models are 16 inches deep rather than the standard 14.

ABOVE LEFT: **An integral-apron acrylic bathtub fits into a three-wall alcove.**
ABOVE: **A modular tub-shower combination is assembled from four key pieces.** BELOW: **Space-efficient recessed tubs and showers come in a wide array of shapes and colors.**

tubs & showers

With or without a step, a corner tub's angle is achieving comfort without compromising floor space.

CORNER TUBS A corner tub is generally a triangular fixture with a finished front and two unfinished sides. However, the term can refer to any tub that's installed in a corner with at least two sides against a wall and one or more decorative sides visible. The boxy white basic bathtub is available in a corner model, with a finished end and one finished side.

A corner tub doesn't have to be triangular. Nearly any type of drop-in tub can be fitted into a platform that covers the exposed sides with custom paneling.

DROP-IN TUBS Drop-in tubs are usually mounted on a platform, but they can be sunken below floor level. Some models overlap the deck; others are undermounted, which makes for easier cleaning and a sleeker look. Because no sides are visible, only the inside of a drop-in tub is finished. Drop-ins are typically made of acrylic or fiberglass-reinforced plastic, which makes them lightweight and able to be manufactured in many colors, but they are also susceptible to scratching and dulling. A plastic tub must be adequately supported from below to compensate for its relative lack of structural integrity. Enameled cast iron, also available for platform installation, is sturdier but may require structural reinforcement because it is so heavy. Drop-in tubs come in a multitude of styles and configurations. Like basic bathtubs, they are made in right- and left-handed versions.

FREESTANDING TUBS Though they are typically built with four legs, some versions of freestanding tubs are made to sit inside a metal or wood frame. Every side of a freestanding tub is visible, so the exterior is completely finished. The most common type of freestanding tub is the perennially popular claw-foot tub. You can buy an original one that's been recon-

A Colonial-style dark wood surround turns this freestanding tub into a striking focal point. Part of the charm comes from the tub's flush undermount design, which conceals the tub's rim beneath the marble top.

ditioned, or look for a new reproduction of a traditional style. Antique tubs are made from cast iron, so be aware that you'll need plenty of muscle to get an old claw-foot into the house, as well as a strong floor to support it. One caveat: If you're mainly a shower person, you may not be happy living with an old-fashioned freestanding tub as your only bathing option. Though you can buy a diverter/showerhead/curtain-rod assembly that will allow you to take showers, such a setup may not do the job as well as a combination tub-shower that's specifically made to perform both functions.

choosing a **whirlpool** tub

Just like conventional bathtubs, whirlpool tubs are available in recessed, corner, drop-in, and freestanding styles. A whirlpool tub can function as a basic bathtub, but it also has motorized circulation jets that provide a soothing hydromassage. Most whirlpools are made for platform installation, but you can get reproduction claw-foot models and even antique bathtubs that have been retrofitted with jets.

When you buy a whirlpool tub, you'll need to know whether you need a right- or left-handed version, and where the

Claw-footed tubs still stand on their own four feet, but new styles have evolved in form and function. Today's models have graceful forms, fanciful hardware, and even whirlpool jets.

This whirlpool bathtub, tucked into a cozy alcove, blasts away the tensions of the day with a generous placement of powerful jets.

pump is located. In most cases, the pump will be opposite the drain, but be sure to check the specific tub you're buying. Some models allow you to choose a remote location for the pump, which reduces the noise factor and makes servicing easier. Whirlpools have become much more reliable in recent years, to the point where jets, air buttons, and air controls are now virtually maintenance-free.

A whirlpool tub can help transform your bathroom into a luxurious home spa, but be prepared to expand your remodel-

ing budget if you buy one. A whirlpool can easily cost twice as much as a basic bathtub, and installation charges will be higher as well. You may need to install special framing, a supplementary water heater just for the tub, or a dedicated electrical circuit to power the pump and controls. In the end, the cost of the whirlpool plus mechanical and structural changes can add significantly to the bottom line. If you plan to make such an investment, here are some factors to consider before you buy:

JETS Whirlpool jets vary quite a bit in design. Some draw water from the bath, then mix it with air and inject it back into the tub. Others simply shoot air into the tub. Air jets are smaller and less powerful than water jets. A conventional whirlpool will have two to eight water jets; a tub that uses air jets may have 10 times as many. Air jets provide a lighter massage, and their blowing action prevents mildew and other moisture-loving substances from accumulating.

How many jets your tub should have, and what kind, is a matter of personal preference. Your decision basically comes down to whether you want a few strong jets or an abundance of softer jets. For a vigorous massage, choose a tub with jets that deliver low-volume, high-pressure spurts. For a gentle, soothing effect, look for high-volume, low-pressure jets.

EXTRA TOUCHES

JETS
Strategically placed jets can relax an aching back and massage tired feet.

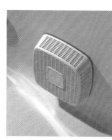

FILTERS
Water circulation systems with suction guards protect against hair entrapment.

SAFETY BARS
Acrylic safety bars offer extra stability while entering or exiting a bathtub.

LIGHTS
Underwater lights come with changeable colored filters that can set a mood.

PILLOWS
Contour pillows are made to be easily adjusted to maximize individual comfort.

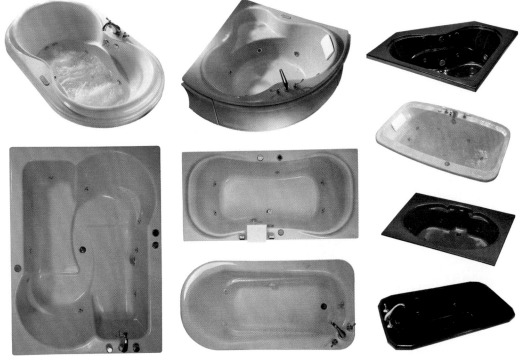

Whirlpool tubs formed from high-gloss acrylic are made in practically every color and shape to suit a multitude of preferences and bathroom layouts.

CONTROLS Some whirlpool tubs have variable-speed pumps with electronic controls that allow you to change from a slow, relaxing massage to a stronger one—a feature that's great in tubs with larger pumps, which can be noisy at high settings. Electronic controls also allow you to set temperatures and cycle times.

SIZE For maximum comfort, you want a tub that's deep enough to maintain an adequate water level. Since whirlpool tubs are generally deeper than conventional bathtubs, you may find that you don't really need an extralong model or one that's made for two people. If you do opt for an oversized tub, make sure your bathroom is prepared to support it. A standard floor is designed to support 40 pounds per square foot. Knowing that water weighs about 8.3 pounds per gallon and 7.5 gallons occupies 1 cubic foot, you can calculate the weight and amount of water required to fill the tub.

EXTRAS The sky's the limit when it comes to accouterments for your whirlpool tub. You can add a built-in phone, stereo, or

TV. Or how about a feature that lets you call your tub and instruct it to fill itself while you're driving home? Even if you're not a gadget lover, you may want a few extras, such as an electronic touchpad or a temperature-programming feature.

An over-the-shoulders waterfall spills a soothing cascade into this luxurious whirlpool bathtub that's built big enough for two.

Almost invisible, this glass shower door swings wide for easy access. The simple, minimalist look is perfect for a small, contemporary space.

One-piece prefabricated shower units, made of high-gloss polyester, are available in several sizes, and with many configurations of benches, grab bars, shelves, and more.

choosing a **shower**

If you have the space for one, a stall shower is an economically sound way to spend your remodeling dollars. According to the National Association of Home Builders, 85 percent of Americans in the market for a home consider a separate shower enclosure an essential or highly desirable bathroom feature. Showers range from prefabricated fiberglass stalls to spacious custom-built rooms lined with tile or stone; for a standard shower stall you'll need at least 36 inches square. Whether you build your shower from scratch or assemble it from manufactured components, you'll have a huge array of sizes, shapes, materials, and colors from which to choose.

PREFABRICATED SHOWER STALLS Single-piece molded showers made of fiberglass, laminate, or synthetic marble offer many advantages. They are watertight, relatively inexpensive, simple to install, and easy to clean. Many include integral soap dishes, grab bars, and other accessories. One-piece showers are usually too large to be installed in a remodeling situation but are often used in new construction. You may be able to use one if you're building an addition or knocking down walls. For a remodel, you can purchase manufactured wall panels and assemble them on-site. These panels lap over a molded shower pan and are then attached to a waterproofed wall. You can get both one-piece and modular showers in square, rectangular, and corner designs.

SHOWER RECEPTORS Unless you're using a one-piece model, your shower will start with a base, sometimes called a receptor or a "pan." You can construct the pan yourself if you have the skills, or purchase one ready-made.

Constructing a traditional mortar-base

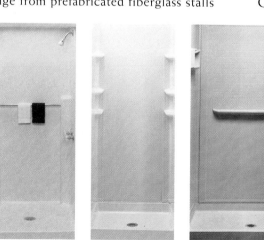

Prefabricated shower pans of high-durability ABS plastic leave the door open for creative surround options.

shower pan requires expert knowledge and skills. The pan must be waterproofed and sloped precisely to the drain, which must be placed at the correct height.

For a simpler installation, you can get prefabricated shower bases in various sizes and shapes. They can be used with manufactured wall panels or with a custom surround. Prefabricated shower pans can be made from molded plastic, cast polymer, solid-surface composite, or poured masonry. Masonry pans often have attractive marble or stone chips throughout.

Make sure that you select a shower pan with a drain opening that will match your existing drainpipe location. You'll also need to determine what kind of entrance threshold you need. Choose a single threshold (one point of entry) if you're going to install the base against three walls. Use a double threshold for a two-wall installation, a triple threshold if the base will abut only one wall.

CUSTOM SHOWERS You can build a custom shower from the ground up, or begin with a prefabricated base—an option that saves loads of time and money. Once your base is in place, you'll need to make sure that adjoining walls are waterproof. This process normally begins with a layer of water-resistant drywall over the studs. The drywall is covered with waterproof cement board and then a finish material such as ceramic tile, slate, granite, marble, or solid surface. When properly installed, even budget tile will last for decades.

SHOWER DOORS Shower doors may swing open, fold back, or pivot. Some are hinged directly to the shower entrance, but most are framed with aluminum. Frames come in many finishes, including epoxy-coated colors, so they can be matched to other bathroom fittings. Doors are made from plastic or tempered glass. Glass, the high-end choice, can be clear, frosted, mirrored, or patterned. Clear doors make the space look most open, but they are difficult to keep clean.

With an airtight shower door and a matching panel above, you can turn your conventional shower into a steam bath by adding a steam generator, which is compact enough to be housed in a cabinet or crawl space.

LEFT: Sliding glass doors are a watertight, relatively inexpensive option for conventionally sized showers and tubs. BELOW: A cascading column of jets offers the ultimate whole-body shower massage in this futuristic aluminum standing spa.

tub & shower fittings

GENERALLY, ONCE YOU INSTALL TUB and shower fittings, it's difficult to change them without considerable work—so it's important to choose them carefully. Quality should be a top priority. Additionally, safety, comfort, and design issues deserve careful consideration.

tub fittings

Tub faucets can be deck- or wall-mounted, and they come in a wide range of styles and finishes to suit the decor of nearly any bathroom. For a unified look, you can choose matching handles for your

Antique silver-trim deck-mount faucet (DETAIL ABOVE) complements a traditionally inspired bathtub.

sink, tub, and shower (see page 99 for more about faucet handles).

The best fittings are made from brass, which costs more than the alternative, plastic, but lasts much longer. Brass faucets are typically finished in chrome, brass, or powder-coated enamel, but you can also get them plated with pewter, nickel, gold, and other specialty finishes such as oil-rubbed bronze. Choose any finish that suits your taste, but be aware some require vigilant upkeep (see page 98 for information on faucet finishes).

Inside every faucet is a valve that controls the flow of water through the spout. Tub and shower valves are concealed behind the bathroom wall, making some repairs difficult and leaks potentially disastrous. For maximum performance and-

ABOVE: **This high-flow ceramic-disc valve turns with a gentle touch and offers automatic control of water temperature. Shower control valves are sold in many different finishes and styles.**

durability, consider spending a bit more for a "washerless" faucet (see page 97 for a discussion of faucet valves). For safety, buy a valve with scald protection (see page 88).

A tub/shower combination requires a diverter valve that switches from one function to the other. An in-wall diverter is controlled by a handle positioned between the two faucets, while a diverter spout has a control button located on the spout itself. A combination tub/shower installation will include a showerhead and shower arm as well as a diverter. Tub-only packages often come with a hand shower—a deck-mounted showerhead attached to the end of a flexible hose. Hand showers are particularly useful for bathing children and dogs, and rinsing dusty house plants and shower walls.

shower fittings

A shower system's command center is the control valve. It turns the water on and off, adjusts the shower temperature, and controls how much water goes to the showerhead and any side sprays. Its capacity determines how many spray options your system can include. If you buy a control valve with scald-protection, it can even keep your shower at a comfortable temperature when someone flushes the toilet or turns on the washing machine (see more about this on page 88).

Today's shower systems offer many ways to get wet. The most popular is still a fixed showerhead installed about 78 inches off the floor and angled to spray at shoulder height. A more versatile option is a hand shower on a slide bar, which can accommodate bathers of different heights. An overhead "shampoo" shower mounted in the ceiling provides a waterfall effect, and can supplement a basic showerhead. Look for a showerhead that has holes in the center as well as around the perimeter for the best spray pattern. Some showerheads have a range of settings that will let you select the

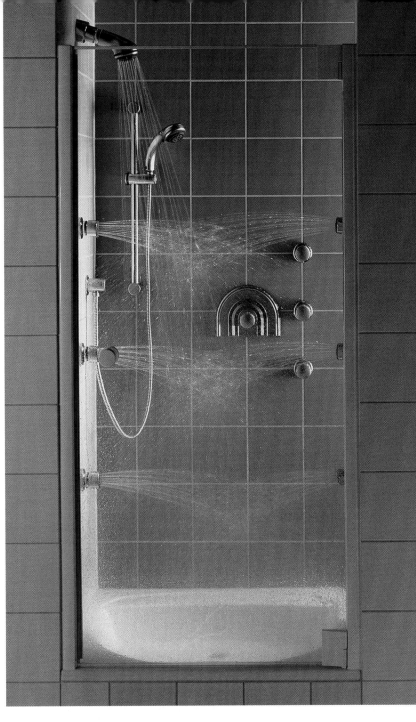

water flow you prefer, from fine spray to coarse, as well as different pulsation levels for a water massage.

Wall-mounted spray jets can be added to a conventional overhead system to create a whole-body shower. These "surround" designs have diverter valves that let you use just a few jets at once, and individual volume controls for each bank of two or three jets. A multispray shower can use 50 gallons of water in eight to ten minutes, so your water bill is likely to go up and you may need a second (or larger) water heater to meet the demand

For a whole-body shower experience, this multihead shower consists of wall-mounted spray jets, a fixed showerhead, and a hand shower, each with its own control valve.

tub & shower fittings

RIGHT: **The showerheads shown here in three popular chrome and brass finishes are equipped with variable spray-stream and volume controls.**

RIGHT TOP: **Dual-head shower arm combines showerhead and body spray in one unit.**
RIGHT BOTTOM: **Oversized adjustable drenching showerhead rains a torrent through over 100 spray channels.**

for longer or consecutive showers. Be sure that the highest jets can be turned off separately so that they won't spray short people in the face. You'll also need a shutoff valve so you can take an ordinary shower if you want to. If you're planning a very elaborate installation, be aware that it can be tricky to coordinate multiple water sources. You may find it worthwhile to have your system professionally designed so you won't be plagued by temperature and pressure fluctuations.

Many cities now require the use of low-flow showerheads in remodels; whether or not one is required, you may want to install this type to reduce your water bill. If you decide to buy a water-saving showerhead, don't try to cut costs: Inexpensive models often deliver a paltry drizzle that cools off as it falls.

SCALD-FREE SHOWERS AND TUBS

A shower or bath faucet that unpredictably spits out scalding-hot water can be a serious hazard. It takes just three seconds for a child to sustain a third-degree burn from water that's heated to 140 degrees Fahrenheit—a typical tap-water temperature in many bathrooms. The simplest scald-prevention measure you can take is to set the thermostat on your water heater at 120 degrees. However, the only way to prevent temperature fluctuations is to install tub and shower valves with built-in scald protection.

Temperature fluctuations are caused by changes in water pressure: When someone flushes the toilet, for example, water pressure drops in the cold-water pipes, altering the mix of hot and cold at the shower or tub. A rapid change in the balance of hot and cold water causes a scalding spray of hot or—if hot-water pressure drops—a chilling blast of cold. To combat this problem, you can install either a pressure-balancing or a thermostatic valve. A pressure-balancing system will automatically adjust the mix of hot and cold water to compensate for changes in water pressure. A thermostatic valve will self-adjust in response to changes in temperature. Some manufacturers offer a control valve that does both. Installation for all of these valves is the same as for a conventional valve.

Most states require the use of pressure-balancing fixtures in new construction. While it's unlikely that you'll be required to use scald-free valves in a bathroom remodel, it makes good sense to take a precaution that's so simple and has so much potential to prevent injuries. Prices are within reach even if you're aiming for a more budget-friendly remodel: Pressure-balancing valves start at less than $100.

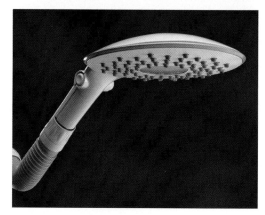

toilets & bidets

THOUGH TOILETS CAN COST ANYwhere from $70 to $1,000, the difference between one model and another is sometimes difficult to discern. But despite their apparent similarities, all commodes are not created equal. Some of the extras you get when you pay more are cosmetic upgrades: retro-style details, colorful finishes, hand-painted designs, specialty flush levers, and the like. Other features will determine how well a toilet flushes and how easy it is to clean and maintain.

Toilets come in one- or two-piece construction. Two-piece toilets have a separate tank and bowl. One-piece, or "low profile," toilets include the tank and bowl in a single unit. A two-piece model will cost less, but a one-piece toilet is easier to clean, and it has no hard-to-clean crevice between the tank and the bowl where leaks can occur. One-piece units often include a seat; most two-piece toilets do not.

Federal law stipulates that any new toilet you buy must use no more than 1.6 gallons of water per flush. That means you'll need to think carefully about what kind of flush system you want. A traditional gravity flush system uses the weight of the water in the toilet tank to generate flushing pressure. This setup worked beautifully in older toilets, which used 3 to 7 gallons of water per flush, but new water-saving gravity-flush toilets are more apt to clog and are less able to rinse the rim of the bowl.

The alternative is a pressure-assisted flush system that uses pressurized air to force water into the bowl. This extra shot of power cuts way down on clogs and the need for multiple flushes, and as a bonus it boosts the toilet's ability to clean itself. Though pressure-assisted flush systems

Form follows function with this two-piece toilet that combines classic styling with a highly efficient flush system.

toilets & bidets

are increasingly popular, they are noisier than conventional toilets and more apt to require repairs. Some models must be plugged into an electrical socket.

Other factors can also affect a toilet's tendency to clog or flush sluggishly. To minimize clogging, look for a larger trapway, the snakelike passage that's behind the bulge in the base of your toilet bowl. Some toilets have a particularly large flush valve—the valve at the inside base of the tank—for the highest possible rate of water flow into the bowl.

The type of toilet bowl you choose is a matter of preference. A round bowl saves space, but many people would rather pay a little more for the comfort of an elongated bowl, which is 2 inches longer and has a larger water surface. The seat must match the shape of the bowl. Seats are available in a variety of materials, including wood, plastic, and polypropylene. Some are cushioned, contoured, or heated for extra comfort.

Before you shop for a toilet, measure the distance from the wall behind the toilet to the center of the toilet drain; this distance is called the rough-in. A 12-inch rough-in is standard, but you might also have a 10- or 14-inch rough-in, depend-

One- and two-piece toilets come in myriad shapes, colors, and styles. Depending on your preferences and needs, you may choose a round bowl or an elongated one for comfort. The mechanical workings vary, too. Models may have any of several kinds of flush valves— including assisted-flush mechanisms—and amenities such as heated seats.

ing on the size of your bathroom. For small baths with very little floor space, you can buy wall-mounted toilets, though they are less commonly available and expensive both to buy and to install. Remember that Lowe's offers convenient, satisfaction-guaranteed professional installation of conventional toilet systems and many other products.

bidets

Bidets, once primarily a European phenomenon, are becoming more common in American bathrooms. A bidet is a personal hygiene fixture that looks rather like a cross between a sink and a toilet. It's equipped with hot and cold water supplies for rinsing. You can choose a vertical spray that rises from the center of the bowl, or a horizontal spray that shoots water over the rim of the bowl. The faucet you choose must match your bidet's spray type. A vertical-spray bidet faucet is mounted on the bidet's deck; a horizontal-style bidet faucet is mounted

on the edge of the bowl. Most bidets have a stopper so that the bowl can be turned into a foot bath or laundry sink. Some have spray jets that rinse the bowl after each use.

A bidet usually costs considerably more than a toilet, but some are priced under $200. If you want a bidet but don't have space for one in your bathroom, you can get a toilet with a bidetlike spray jet.

bathroom sinks

TODAY'S BATHROOM SINKS (ALSO called "lavatories" or "lavs") come in such a variety of configurations that you can outfit any bathroom with ease. There are tiny wall-hung versions for the powder room, classic pedestals for the old-fashioned family bath, and elaborate dual-basin models for the master suite.

This stylish, easy-care pedestal sink, with its small footprint, is perfect for a diminutive bathroom.

With a multitude of colors and materials to choose from, you can evoke any mood you like: stainless steel or solid-surface resins for a contemporary look, vitreous china or enameled cast iron for a traditional one, or perhaps glass or copper for a more theatrical quality. At Lowe's you can even order a composite sink that's custom-colored to match your towels or your tile.

Before you shop for sinks, refer to the Project Workbook, beginning on page 134, for information on planning your bathroom. Do you need two sinks? Extra storage? Easy upkeep? Keep in mind how much wear and tear your sink will have to endure. If you're remodeling a seldom-used powder room, a budget-friendly but scratch-prone fiberglass sink or a delicate hand-painted ceramic one may be just fine; for the family bathroom, you'll probably want something more durable.

Come to the store armed with exact measurements and a rough idea of what you'd like to spend. Your Lowe's Plumbing Sales Specialist can help you find a sink that fits your space, your lifestyle, and your budget. When you're close to making a decision, consider faucet options; many lavatory sinks have predrilled holes for mounting a faucet, so your choices have to be compatible.

deck-mounted sinks

Because they allow for maximum storage and counter space and suit an enormous range of decorating styles, deck-mounted

sculptural freestanding basins can perch on the slimmest of vanities, adding counter space and storage without sacrificing floor space. They are usually paired with space-saving wall-mounted fittings.

Deck-mounts are available in a wide variety of materials, with prices varying accordingly: A fiberglass-reinforced plastic basin may sell for less than a hundred dollars, while a hand-hammered copper one may cost a few thousand. The options you'll see most often are fiberglass, enameled steel, vitreous china, and enameled cast iron. Each has its advantages and drawbacks. Fiberglass and enameled steel are affordable but tend to show signs of wear and tear. Vitreous china weighs more and costs more, but it does a better job of resisting scratches and stains, and it can be molded and painted for a highly ornamental effect. Enameled cast iron has a smooth, elegant finish that lasts longest of all, but it is also the heaviest and most expensive of the lot.

If you're searching for something more unusual, you can find deck-mounted sinks made from stainless steel, brass, nickel, and even crystal. Such materials look elegant, but they can be expensive and difficult to maintain; brass and copper, for example, can tarnish.

TOP LEFT: Clearly contemporary, this deck-mounted glass basin catches the flow from a sweeping chrome wall-mount faucet. BOTTOM LEFT: A dark vitreous china undermount sink allows for an uninterrupted top on this handsome hardwood vanity.

BELOW: Self-rimming sinks, the easiest type to install in a counter-top, are offered in a broad palette of colors, shapes, and styles.

sinks remain popular year after year. A deck-mounted basin can be set into or on top of a vanity, a cabinet, or even a free-standing frame. Most deck-mounts are made to sit inside a countertop cutout.

Drop-in sinks can be mounted in a variety of ways. The self-rimming variety, which overlaps the countertop, is simplest to install but tends to collect dirt where the edges of the sink and the countertop meet. For easier cleanup, choose an undermount sink, which is mounted to the underside of the countertop.

For a stylish alternative, check out deck-mounted sinks that sit on top of the counter—so-called above-counter sinks (see pages 16, 23, 43, 51, and 54). These

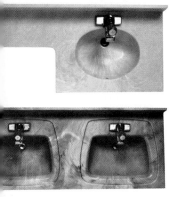

Integral-bowl sinks, made in many configurations, seamlessly combine countertop and bowl for easy care.

For an interesting, decorative effect, this solid-surface combination marries an almond-toned counter with a white sink.

integral-bowl sinks

Another type of sink is the integral-bowl sink, where basin and countertop are a single piece that's attractive and easy to install and maintain.

Integral-bowl sinks are most often made from solid-surface materials, but they also come in vitreous china, fiberglass, concrete, and cast polymers such as cultured marble and cultured granite. Solid-surface materials are relatively expensive, but they offer many advantages. From a practical point of view, they're ideally suited to the bathroom: They withstand just about any insult except for extreme direct heat, and they can be repaired if nicked or scratched. Solid-surface units come in a wide range of colors and patterns—match the sink to the countertop, or use contrasting colors and decorative borders.

If a solid-surface model is beyond your budget, a cultured marble integral-bowl sink will be more affordable, although less durable. At many retailers, such as Lowe's, you can buy a cultured-marble unit and take it home on the same day; custom-color and solid-surface versions are available by special order. When shopping for a one-piece sink, make sure you choose one that's deep enough; some are so shallow that you'll get sprayed when the faucet's running full force.

This pedestal sink's curves complement a contemporary bathroom.

pedestal sinks

A pedestal sink is perfectly suited to a small bath or powder room. Its small footprint occupies a minimal amount of floor space, and its slender silhouette lends an open, airy feeling to its surroundings. Even if space isn't at a premium, a pedestal sink's classic good looks make it a winner when your bathroom plan calls for a traditional decor.

A pedestal sink consists of two pieces: a basin, which is mounted to the wall, and a stand, or pedestal, which is secured to the floor and usually conceals all or some of the plumbing. The vast majority of pedestal sinks are made of vitreous china, which makes them durable and easy to clean but often limits your color choices to various shades of white. Other options, such as stainless steel and several shades of fireclay (similar to vitreous china), are available by special order. Although some versions are expensive, most pedestal sinks provide plenty of elegance at prices that are reasonable.

Pedestal sinks can be tricky to install.

bathroom sinks

Measurements must be precise, and it's often a challenge to fit the plumbing inside the pedestal. If you're replacing a deck-mounted sink, you may need to move water lines and repair the floor and walls. Remember, too, that a pedestal sink provides no storage area below the basin and no countertop around it. If you opt for one, you'll need to compensate for the lost space by installing shelves, a medicine cabinet, or other storage nearby.

wall-mounted sinks

A wall-mounted sink is even more compact than its closest relation, the pedestal sink. Because it requires no base, it liberates floor space and slips neatly into the tightest spots. Some diminutive models can even be tucked into the corner of a tiny powder room.

As the term implies, a wall-mounted sink is fastened directly to the wall with hangers or angle brackets. Wall-mounted basins are most often made of white vitreous china, with a retro look that is just right for a traditional-style bathroom. However, flashy new models featuring materials such as stainless steel, brass, and brushed nickel are increasingly available. Though high-style versions can be pricey, wall-mounted sinks are usually among the least expensive on the market.

A wall-mounted sink must be adequately supported. If you're installing one for the first time, be sure to reinforce the wall behind it.

ABOVE: **From classic to contemporary, the elegant forms of pedestal sinks can set the stage for the entire look of a bathroom.**

FAR LEFT: **A decorative enameled-cast-iron sink, with elaborate basin scrollwork, evokes the elegance of a Victorian fountain.** LEFT: **A contemporary wall-mounted sink fits in flawlessly with traditionally styled bathroom decor.**

bathroom sinks

A new take on a venerable classic, this console table with leather-covered legs contributes a decidedly masculine look.

console sinks

A console sink offers all the attractions of a pedestal sink and then some. Its expanded deck, set atop furniture-like legs, provides plenty of room for soap and other sundries. Its open configuration creates a feeling of spaciousness and frees up wall space so you can showcase a beautiful paint color or wallpaper.

A console sink can give your bathroom a vintage look; some manufacturers even offer reproductions of antique consoles. But you can find all kinds of variations on the classic design. Though porcelain or ceramic legs are common, consoles come with chrome, wood, bronze, wrought iron, stainless steel, and even rattan legs. For the traditional vitreous china basin, you can substitute marble, stainless steel, solid-surface materials, or glass. High-end and custom models can be equipped with dual basins and storage space below.

	ADVANTAGES	DISADVANTAGES
DECK-MOUNTED	▪ Ample counter space ▪ Storage below ▪ Array of materials and mounting options	▪ May not fit in tight spaces ▪ Added expense for countertop, cabinet, and installation
INTEGRAL-BOWL	▪ Custom look ▪ Ample counter and storage space ▪ Easy to clean and install ▪ Wide selection of materials, including solid-surface acrylics, cast polymers, vitreous china, fiberglass, and concrete	▪ Some are costly ▪ Basin may be too shallow
PEDESTAL	▪ Fits in small space ▪ No cabinets or countertop to buy or install ▪ Style appropriate for traditional decor ▪ Easy to clean	▪ No counter space ▪ No storage ▪ Limited choice of materials and colors
WALL-MOUNTED	▪ Compact ▪ Affordable ▪ A good style for older homes or ones with traditional decor	▪ No storage or counter space ▪ Requires addition of wall support ▪ Somewhat limited choice of materials and colors
CONSOLE	▪ Wider deck can replace counter space ▪ Vintage look is stylish	▪ May not fit in small area ▪ May require a special order

bathroom faucets

WHEN IT'S TIME TO EQUIP YOUR SINK with a new faucet, you'll find a huge array of styles and prices. How do you choose the right one for your remodel? Price is a good measure of faucet quality, and you should certainly buy the best faucet you can afford. But you also need a faucet that suits your taste and fits your sink.

When you shop for faucets, you'll have four basic styles from which to choose. Centerset faucets, made for predrilled sinks, combine a spout and valves on a single base unit. Single-lever faucets have one handle that's often part of the spout. Widespread faucet components are each mounted separately, so the spout and handles sit directly on the sink or countertop instead of a base. Wall-mounted faucets, as the name implies, are installed in the wall.

Bathroom vanity and pedestal sinks are designed for centerset, single-lever, and widespread faucets. Wall-mounted faucets are typically paired with above-counter and freestanding basins that require a long spout. Many sinks have predrilled holes on 4-inch or 8-inch centers; if yours does, you'll need to make sure that your faucet matches your sink's hole configuration. Single-lever faucets are an exception, since they can be modified with a cover plate that will conceal the extra openings.

Each type of faucet has its attractions. Centerset faucets are widely available and usually more affordable than other styles. Single-control faucets are handy—the only kind that meet the criteria for uni-

versal design (see page 62)—and suited to a contemporary decor. Widespread sets offer flexible placement, but you'll pay a premium for the styling—as much as twice the price of a comparable centerset.

faucet construction

When you're comparing faucets, it definitely pays to keep in mind the old adage that beauty is only skin deep. Every faucet has an inner valve that controls water flow through the spout. The quality of that valve is what determines how drip-free, reliable, and durable your faucet will be.

CLOCKWISE FROM TOP LEFT: The four primary faucet types include a classic European-style widespread faucet set, minimalist wall-mount, dual-handle centerset, and easy-to-operate single-lever model.

bathroom faucets

Compression-valve faucets are the least expensive on the market and have been in use the longest. They operate by means of a stem that rises and falls to open and close the water's passageway. Compression faucets begin to drip when the washer at the base of the stem wears out.

For better performance and reliability, it's worth paying a little more for a "washerless" faucet. You have three options:

Cartridge faucets use rubber O-rings inside a cylindrical cartridge to control the flow of water. These midpriced faucets are very reliable, especially if equipped with a brass cartridge, and leaks can usually be repaired with a simple,

With its sparkling chrome finish, this sleek widespread faucet has a very contemporary look.

A low-profile widespread faucet with an oil-rubbed bronze finish gives this sink a soft, antiqued feel.

Polished chrome and brass detailing intermingle to give this solid-cast brass faucet a custom appearance.

inexpensive O-ring replacement.

Ball faucets have a rotating metal or plastic ball that regulates the amount of incoming water. The valve has just one moving part, which reduces the chances of malfunction. A plastic ball will eventually wear out, but a metal ball is designed to last a lifetime. If the ball needs to be replaced, the cost is low.

Ceramic-disc faucets, first popularized by high-end European manufacturers, are ultradurable and nearly maintenance-free. They employ two fire-hardened ceramic discs that move against each other in a shearing action, blocking water or allowing it to pass through; the seal is watertight because the discs are polished to near-perfect flatness. The precise ergonomic control you get with a ceramic-disc faucet is a boon for children and arthritis sufferers. Ceramic discs are used primarily in mid-range and high-end faucets. Repair entails replacing the ceramic-disc cartridge, which costs $15 to $25.

Check the warranty on your faucet before you buy. The best offer lifetime protection against leaks and drips.

materials and finishes

Though faucets vary dramatically in appearance, most are made from brass. Brass parts are machine-fabricated or cast in molds (the better of the two methods), then given a finish such as chrome, brass plating, or powder-coated enamel. The finish is what makes one faucet look different from another.

Polished chrome is the most popular bathroom-faucet finish. It suits any decor and is exceedingly durable when manufactured with high nickel content. It's easy to wipe clean, but water spots reappear quickly; brushed chrome is easier to keep spot-free. Brass-plated faucets look striking but can be difficult to maintain. If you want a high-gloss brass finish, you can spare yourself the ordeal of bimonthly polishing sessions by choosing a faucet with a factory-applied clear coat; some of

these are virtually unscratchable as well. Powder-coated enamel comes in a wide range of decorator colors that are electrostatically applied and baked on, providing a durable finish that should last as long as the faucet. You can also choose gold plate, pewter, or nickel finishes.

Faucet finishes are part of the look of a bathroom. Nickel, pewter, brass, porcelain, and brushed-metal finishes will complement a traditional decor, while enameled and high-gloss finishes have a more contemporary look.

Some manufacturers offer better finishes only in their higher-priced models, but others use the same finishing process for all of their faucets, including their more competitively priced offerings.

other considerations

Faucet handles and spouts come in a variety of styles. Each one will give your bathroom a different look: Cross-shaped handles and gooseneck spouts, for example, set an old-fashioned tone, whereas a single-handle lever faucet has a more modern appearance. In addition to style, you should consider who will be using the faucet—cross handles can be difficult for some people to turn, while lever handles are easier to operate.

Special features you may want to consider include a high-tech faucet that displays a digital temperature readout and one that shuts off automatically when you're done washing your hands. You can add a drinking spout, a soap dispenser, or even a gum-massage attachment. Many such offerings are indispensable only to die-hard gadget devotees. However, if you have young children, it's worth considering a scald-guard or temperature-limit feature. Available in single-control faucets, a scald-guard feature allows you to remove the handle and adjust the maximum water temperature.

countertops

IN ANY BATHROOM, YOU NEED A countertop that can stand up to splashes, steam, spilled cosmetics, and a host of other challenges. The good news is many countertop surfaces on the market today can handle the job with style. You'll discover hundreds of options, from materials that require professional installers—such as those put in by Lowe's installation services—to products you can deal with yourself during a weekend.

LAMINATE Affordable, easy to install, and available in a huge range of colors and patterns, plastic laminate is the most popular surface for bath countertops. Its smooth surface is easy to clean, but it can accumulate scratches, stains, and chips over time, and—once damaged—it's virtually impossible to repair. When you're shopping for laminates, keep in mind that high-gloss finishes show smudges, and seams of standard types are visible. Laminate countertops can be built up from particleboard and sheet laminate or purchased ready-made with an integrated

RIGHT: **Durable high-pressure laminates come in many shades and colors, including this soft, natural green.** BELOW: **A cultured-marble countertop with integral sink and back-splash is a good choice for a limited budget.**

backsplash. Ready-made "postformed" versions require gluing the laminate onto particleboard, a challenge for even an experienced do-it-yourselfer.

CAST POLYMER Cultured marble (also called synthetic marble) and other cast polymers are another option if you're looking for a countertop surface that's easy on the budget. Cast-polymer countertops are commonly sold with an integral sink. Some can be combined with a matching tub and shower. The chief disadvantage of cast polymers is that they are less durable than other materials. Quality varies from one manufacturer to another, since cast polymers are often made in small shops, so check for Cultured Marble Institute or IAPMO certification.

This glazed porcelain tile re-creates the rustic elegance of hand-carved travertine. Tile is extremely durable and easy to clean.

CERAMIC TILE Tile makes a handsome, water-resistant countertop that works with any decor, from contemporary to French country. There are literally thousands of colors and textures to choose from, some featuring raised, recessed, or painted designs. Prices vary from $1 or $2 a square foot to many times that amount, depending mostly on whether the product is mass-produced or hand-made. Fortunately, even a budget-tile countertop will last for many years if properly installed. If you're trying to control costs, keep your countertop simple and add a few designer tiles to your back-splash. Though tile itself is easy to clean, grout lines can gather dirt and bacteria. To minimize this problem, keep grout lines thin and regular.

SOLID-SURFACE MATERIALS Solid-surface products such as those with the trade names Corian, Surell, and Fountainhead are nonporous and stain resistant, making them ideal for bathroom use. A solid-surface countertop and basin can be created as a single piece, resulting in a seamless unit that's easy to clean. Solid surfaces come in hundreds of colors with both matte and polished finishes, and you can add patterns and decorative borders. Repairs are easy—scratches and stains can be sanded away—but installation is best left to a professional. Though they're costly (up to $170 per linear foot), solid-surface materials may be within reach if your bathroom is small.

BELOW: This solid-surface, single-piece countertop-and-bowl combination is sleek and simple in both looks and maintenance.

countertops

NATURAL STONE Though it is not the toughest or most maintenance-free surface, natural stone remains popular because of its rich, varied appearance. Granite, the most common choice for stone countertops, is water-resistant, heatproof, and basically impossible to scratch, but it can absorb stains. Marble, the standard of elegance for centuries, is vulnerable to scratching as well as staining. Both marble and limestone can be damaged by oil, alcohol, acid—and even the chemicals in some tap water. You can avoid many of these problems by sealing a marble or limestone countertop on a regular basis and without fail (ask for products that are specially formulated for use on stone).

When you're figuring out how much your project will cost, keep in mind that you'll have to purchase an entire slab of stone to have a countertop fabricated to your specifications (you may be able to use the leftovers for a tabletop or vanity). For a small countertop, you may be able to use a partial slab, known as a remnant, which sells for much less. For an even more economical alternative, check out the selection of stone tiles.

ENGINEERED STONE A new twist in solid-surface technology is engineered stone, a mixture of natural quartz and silica sand combined under extreme pressure at very high temperatures. Engineered stone can be made to look like granite, marble, or travertine, but it is more durable. It resists stains, mildew, and bacterial growth, and it has the strength of granite with four times the flexibility, which makes it less likely to crack. Available in a variety of colors, patterns, and finishes, slabs are produced in three standard thicknesses. Its manufactured surface is completely uniform, so there's never a problem keeping a consistent look between countertop and backsplash pieces.

OTHER MATERIALS If you're inclined to take the road less traveled, you may want to explore some of the other available countertop options.

RIGHT: **A black granite countertop complements a brushed-nickel faucet set and painted maple console.** BELOW: **Luxurious quartzlike solid surfacing ties together the elements of this bathroom, from the multilevel countertop to the shower walls.**

Stainless steel is nonporous, resistant to heat, and holds up well in wet areas. Be sure to purchase thick sheets (at least 16-gauge) of genuine stainless steel made from a chromium/nickel blend (imitations will stain), and be prepared to live with water spots and scratches.

Specialty metals such as copper and zinc make a very striking countertop, and they resist denting despite their softness. They scratch easily and must be polished regularly to retain their bright finish. For lower maintenance and a different appearance, they can be left to oxidize, causing them to develop a rich patina.

Concrete has a handmade look that works well with other natural elements such as slate and wood. Cast in forms or molds either in a shop or on site, concrete must be properly sealed periodically to resist stains. Over time it is likely to change color and it may develop visible hairline cracks.

Wood makes a beautiful furniturelike countertop—in fact, a piece of furniture such as a dresser can make a striking vanity for a drop-in sink. However, the tendency of most woods to warp, split, and mildew when they get wet repeatedly makes wood an impractical choice for all but the most vigilant housekeepers. If the drawbacks don't deter you, give your wood countertop a fighting chance by preparing it with multiple coats of sealant, wiping the surface dry after every use, and polishing regularly.

backsplashes

A backsplash isn't a mandatory accompaniment to a countertop, but you may want one (if you've chosen a laminate or solid-surface countertop it will probably come with an integral backsplash). As its name implies, the function of a backsplash is to protect the wall from splashes and stains. Any durable, water-resistant surface will do; the most obvious course of action is to use the same material you select for your countertop.

The backsplash is the ideal place to express your creativity. Since you'll need very little finish material, you can splurge on handmade tiles or any other indulgence that strikes your fancy. Install your backsplash last so that you can easily accommodate electrical outlets, switches, and the like.

If you prefer to keep it simple and save money, you can omit the backsplash completely. A high-quality semigloss paint or properly applied scrubbable wallpaper will offer perfectly adequate water and stain resistance for most bathroom walls. It's usually best to paint or paper the wall after installing your countertop.

CLOCKWISE FROM TOP LEFT: A ceramic tile backsplash features decorative accent border tiles with a stonelike look. Metallic-finish mosaic wall tiles create a gleaming, mirrored backsplash. This durable laminate countertop has an integral backsplash with a waterfall edge.

bathroom storage

THE BATHROOM CAN EASILY BECOME a clutter magnet. Without a well-planned storage system, even the most beautiful remodel may soon be buried in hairbrushes, hotel-size toiletries, and countless other forms of bathroom flotsam.

Some solutions to this potential problem cost little or nothing. For starters, before you begin your remodel, reduce the amount of stuff that needs to be stored: Retire threadbare towels, clear away cosmetics you haven't used in six months, find another place for medicines (they shouldn't be stored in the bathroom because humidity can damage them), and consider moving seldom-needed items such as elastic bandages out of the room. After you've taken inventory of what's

A weathered-white vanity and tall apothecary cabinet, both with antiqued bronze hardware, set a classic style in this roomy bathroom.

left, search your floor plan for opportunities to add storage space during construction. A half-wall that conceals plumbing can function as a shelf. A room divider can work overtime as a storage unit with built-in nooks for towels, personal-grooming supplies, or even a TV. You can fit a niche between two studs, or extend your countertop above the toilet tank.

Your plan will probably include cabinets as well, and they should be ordered before you begin construction. There are two basic styles to choose from: traditional American cabinets with a faceframe covering the edges of each box, or "European-style" frameless cabinets edged with a simple trim strip. Both types are manufactured and sold in a variety of ways. Stock cabinets, which are mass-produced in standard sizes and configura-

tions, can accommodate limited budgets and tight schedules; their less-costly cousins, ready-to-assemble cabinets, are sold knocked down in flat boxes and put together on site. Custom cabinets built from scratch take longer to arrive and cost at least five times more, but a skilled craftsman can turn out quality woodwork that no machine can match. Semi-custom cabinets can offer the best of both worlds, allowing you to order special sizes, configurations, or finishes without breaking the bank.

Even stock cabinets come in a wide range of dimensions designed to make the most of limited bathroom space. Generously proportioned vanities provide more counter area than ever before. Tall cabinets and floor-to-ceiling towers put vertical space to work. For especially

ABOVE: **A selection of wall-mounted medicine cabinets includes, from the top down, an oak cabinet with shelf and towel bar; stainless-steel sliding door cabinet with a lighted frame; swing-door cabinet with thinly framed mirror.**
RIGHT: **Floor-to-ceiling storage towers flank a three-piece mirror vanity set in white laminate.**

vanity cabinets Stock and semi-custom vanity cabinets are sold in a wide variety of sizes, styles, and configurations. Standard widths are 24, 30, 36, 48, and 60 inches; heights range from 31 to 33½ inches and depths are normally either 18 or 21 inches. Hardwood and laminates are the most durable surfaces; high-quality wood cabinets utilize a combination of solid hardwood and panels.

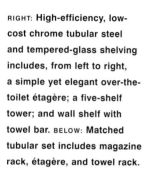

RIGHT: **High-efficiency, low-cost chrome tubular steel and tempered-glass shelving includes, from left to right, a simple yet elegant over-the-toilet étagère; a five-shelf tower; and wall shelf with towel bar.** BELOW: **Matched tubular set includes magazine rack, étagère, and towel rack.**

tight spots, there are ultraslim and corner configurations. Many designs incorporate mirrors and lighting, and you can buy coordinating accessories, as well as matching paneling for facing your whirlpool or drop-in bathtub. Finishes run the gamut from easy-clean laminate to solid hardwood. For a sophisticated look, choose a cabinet line with architectural details such as crown molding and fluted panels.

Most manufacturers offer a range of accessories that let you customize your cabinet interiors to suit your needs. You can get interior components such as pull-out bins, lazy-Susans, and removable built-in laundry hampers that make it easy to transport clothes to the washer. Even "wasted" space can be transformed with a few additions: Put tilt-out storage under the sink, or house a slide-out platform in the toe-kick of your vanity to help children reach the sink.

An effective bathroom plan will include a mix of cabinets and other storage options. Shelving is a practical, affordable alternative that's ideal for displaying decorative objects and keeping toiletries close at hand; for an open, airy feeling, choose transparent glass shelves that let light shine through. A row of apothecary drawers makes a perfect organizer for small items such as hair clips and cotton balls, and it doubles as a storage ledge. If you have a pedestal or wall-mounted sink, an old-fashioned medicine cabinet can make up for the loss of undersink storage space.

Freestanding storage units offer convenience and flexibility: They're usually sold on a cash-and-carry basis, and they can be moved (or removed) without expensive demolition and repairs. Many versions, including étagères and stand-alone bath towers, consume very little floor space. Some are equipped with wheels for maximum versatility—in a small bath, you might want to try a portable trolley that can be wheeled alongside the tub when you bathe and tucked away in a corner afterwards. When you're considering your bathroom storage options, keep in mind that furniture made for the kitchen or bedroom can provide a perfect place for storing towels and toiletries. For example, a stainless-steel prep table or bar cart would be perfect for a contemporary bathroom; and an antique or reproduction armoire would fit in well in a traditional one.

HOW AND WHERE TO STORE BATH ITEMS

Deciding how much space you'll need is only part of planning a bathroom storage system. You'll also have to determine exactly what kinds of storage to include.

Start by going through your belongings. First, consider items that you use every day. These should be stored within reach. You might want to install some easy-access open shelving so you won't have to tug at doors and drawers when you're in a hurry. Though you may be tempted, avoid using the countertop, sink deck, or rim of the tub as storage space.

Many objects can be situated according to function. Towels should be kept near the bath, toilet paper within reach of the commode. Articles that are purely decorative are best placed at eye level.

Rarely used items can be stored on high shelves, in bins at the back of cabinets, or boxes in the back of drawers. Some items may be better off in a remote location where they won't be occupying scarce bathroom space. However, don't banish the extra soap and shampoo that you may need when you're in midshower.

Keep in mind safety as well as convenience when you plan your storage. Bath toys should be stored close to floor level so children don't fall while reaching for them; use a corner stand, low shelves, or a net that drips into the tub. Heavy or sharp items should not be stored where they can fall and cause injuries. Cleaning supplies should be kept in high cabinets that are inaccessible to children—many products are highly poisonous and should be behind a locked door. If you are keeping medicine in the bathroom, put it above the reach of children and in a place that can be locked.

Easily assembled wood-and-glass cabinets provide excellent storage and style on a budget. Several types are available, including over-the-toilet, wall-mounted, and standing cabinetry.

bath accessories

THOUGH THEY'RE OFTEN AN AFTER-thought, accessories are in fact central to the success of a bathroom remodel. The right details set the tone for a room and give it a polished, pulled-together look. Happily, bath accessories come in a huge array of styles and finishes to help you evoke any mood you want to create. Many product lines allow you to coordinate all your bathroom hardware, from towel bars to toothbrush holders. Some can even be matched to faucet handles, sinks, and tubs.

Before you shop for accessories, make a list of what you'll need. Towel bars, a mirror, and a toilet-paper holder are obvious; you may also want robe hooks, towel rings, switch plates, shower shelves, soap dishes, a toothbrush holder, or a hotel-style rack that includes two or three

ABOVE: **This towel holder curves grace-fully with hand-wrought European styling.** RIGHT: **Hammered-bronze cabinet pulls and antique-style soap and lotion dispensers lend a hearty country look to this casual bath.**

LEFT: Simple details such as soap and cup holders, towel rack, and lighting work in unison to set a relaxed tone reminiscent of a New England seaside cottage. BELOW: Cabinet knobs and pulls are sold in myriad shapes, styles, and materials suited to nearly any bathroom's personality. For more information about cabinets, see pages 104–109.

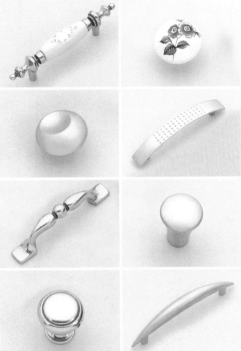

RIGHT: The handsome cast-metal knobs and pulls on these semi-custom cabinets are the perfect complement to the warm taupe glazed-wood finish and green-toned counters.

bath accessories

towel bars and a shelf. For a luxurious touch, you can add a towel warmer that will double as a bathroom heater.

Look over your floor plan to determine where hardware should be placed. Don't forget that you can install bars, hooks, and rings on the end of a cabinet, the back of a door, the front of a vanity, or just about anywhere that won't interfere

with doors, electrical outlets, or heating vents. Note where studs are located, for secure attachment (see pages 115 and 218–219). And don't forget that a heated towel bar will need access to electricity.

Most bath hardware is made from covered brass; common finishes are chrome and brass plating. There are also plastic, wood, and ceramic versions. Get the best accessories you can afford. Even high-end hardware won't dramatically increase your remodeling budget, and its finish will last a lot longer than cheaper products. Stick to solid-brass construction with a bit of heft, and avoid plastic unless your bathroom will be very gently used.

Select a group of amenities that goes well together and blends with the rest of your bathroom fixtures and fittings. If you can't match finishes exactly, look for similar textures. High-gloss finishes will

Soap and lotion dispensers, in finishes and styles that match almost any faucet set, eliminate countertop clutter and mess.

Aged-bronze towel ring, towel bar, robe hook, and toilet-paper rod set a formal yet rugged tone.

Scroll-etched pewter toilet-paper holder, clothes hooks, towel bar, light switch, and electrical plates dazzle a bathroom with a hand-wrought look.

Space motifs on cabinet pulls, toilet-paper rod, and towel bars add a whimsical touch to a child's bath.

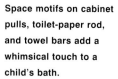

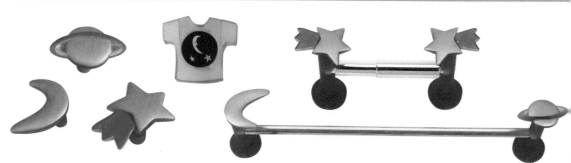

RIGHT: The smooth curves of these rounded ceramic accessories, reminiscent of a barber's shaving brush, lend turn-of-the-century charm to a bathroom.

This ceramic cup holder's bright white tone and rounded lines provide a simple but interesting contrast to the dark blue square wall tiles.

An inset ceramic toilet paper holder takes advantage of the hollow space inside a wall to recess the roll. This must be placed between—not directly over—wall studs.

This white ceramic wall-mounted soap dish stands ready and waiting to serve up the soap.

A matching robe hook with bulbous rounded edges promises to hang tough without tearing towels or clothing.

complement a contemporary-style bathroom. Brushed finishes tend to look more traditional; however, polished brass is a historically accurate choice for a Victorian or Craftsman bath, and polished chrome will replicate the look of polished nickel, which was the standard for bathroom installations from the turn of the century until the mid-1930s.

Note that some ceramic accessories are made to be installed right into a tiled wall, so be sure to have these on hand before you begin tiling; hardware that's meant to be screwed into plaster or drywall can be selected at the end of the construction process.

One accessory—a mirror—is both a necessity and a design element in a bath-

bath accessories

room because its reflective surface amplifies existing light and makes the room seem more spacious. For practical reasons, the bathroom mirror is best placed above the sink, where activities such as shaving take place. Select the largest mirror that will fit—preferably one that provides a clear view of the face and upper body. You'll find ready-to-hang mirrors in a variety of standard sizes at home improvement centers such as Lowe's. If you need a nonstandard size, you can have a local retailer cut a mirror to your specifications. You'll pay at least twice as much for a custom mirror, and the price will be even higher if you add beveled edges or a custom frame. Whichever

Clipped corners and a dark finish give this solid mahogany-framed mirror handsome American Colonial style.

Architectural details like crown molding and a beveled mirror distinguish this classic medicine cabinet.

A dark wood–framed mirror, along with antique decorations, supplies the feel of turn-of-the-century Americana.

This richly detailed recessed cabinet complements any of several design styles, from contemporary to retro to Art Deco.

option you choose, make sure your bathroom mirror is adequately illuminated (see page 125 for information about bathroom lighting). If your budget and your space allow, you may want to consider supplementing a standard above-sink mirror with an optical makeup mirror or a shaving mirror for the shower.

Last but not least is the humble shower curtain, which typically hangs from a rod that attaches to two walls with screws or that is spring-loaded to fit tightly against the walls. A shower curtain is not only the most economical option for enclosing your tub or shower stall, it's the most flexible. Equipped with pockets, it can hold bath toys or shampoo bottles. It can be a neutral backdrop for your bathroom design, or it can provide a colorful counterpoint to plain walls and fixtures. In addition, when you tire of it, it is easily and inexpensively replaced.

To help prevent the curtain from mildewing, pull it out of the tub when you're done showering and spread it out so that it will dry quickly. When your shower curtain finally wears out, it can gain new purpose as a drop cloth for painting or as a spill catcher under baby's high chair.

To install bath accessories, use toggle bolts rather than plastic wall anchors. Grab bars and fixtures that will be jostled a great deal should be screwed directly to wall studs. If that's not possible, you may have to cut open the wall and install 1-by-4 backing to provide a solid anchor. Mirrors should be mounted above a backsplash or a few inches above the counter to reduce the risk of moisture damaging the backing. Installation of a custom mirror is best left to a professional unless you're a skilled do-it-yourselfer.

Inexpensive chromed-wire accessories can add function—and a little style—to the bath. CLOCKWISE FROM TOP LEFT: Tub caddy; hooks for hangables; corner ledge caddy; showerhead caddy; suction-cup corner caddy.

shower curtains
Made from fabric or plastic, ready-made shower curtains typically cost between $10 and $50, but some, usually custom-made, sell for hundreds of dollars. At the top end you get fashion but not necessarily more durability. Curtains made of plastic or cotton duck are watertight and can be used alone. Other fabric curtains must be paired with a liner of vinyl or quick-dry fabric.

bathroom flooring

BATHROOM FLOORING SHOULD BE waterproof, washable, skid-resistant, and, of course, attractive. Many materials can meet these requirements; choosing one for your remodel is a matter of finding the mix of fashion, function, and affordability that's right for you.

Vinyl continues to be the most common material for bathroom flooring because of its low price, high durability, and easy upkeep. But other options abound.

Ceramic tile has been popular for decades, thanks to its toughness and classic good looks. "Natural" materials such as linoleum and upscale ones such as granite are gaining on synthetic lookalikes. Newer laminate and wood products are being adapted to bathrooms, and even carpet is showing up in grooming centers, dressing rooms, and other special-purpose areas of the master suite.

Before you shop for flooring, you'll need to measure your bathroom and create a scale drawing (see page 138 for information on drawing an existing floor plan). Take this with you to the store so your flooring specialist can help you make your selection and place an accurate order. Flooring is sold in varying widths, so when you're pricing it, be sure to convert your square-yardage number to the specific dimensions of each product to determine the total cost.

Though your taste should guide you through the shopping process, don't make a purchase until you're certain that the product you like is also suited to the space you're remodeling. The first factor to consider is whether your bathroom is on grade (ground level), above grade, or below grade. Some products should not be installed on grade-level or basement floors because of potential moisture problems, so be sure to ask your flooring specialist if your selection will work in the location you have in mind.

Sheet vinyl is practical, easy-care flooring; this handsome tile-like pattern comes with a lifetime wear warranty.

Consider as well what kind of subflooring your new floor will need. If your base is a concrete slab, you can choose almost any type, but a wood subfloor may not support a stone or ceramic-tile installation unless you add support (see page 200). You may be able to install your new flooring on top of an existing floor, as long as it's sturdy (have a large adult jump on it to make sure it doesn't flex), free of dips, and level. But beware of adding too many layers: A floor that's more than ½ inch higher than the abutting floor could pose a tripping hazard.

Finally, determine how your new floor will blend with your overall decorating scheme and the rest of the flooring in your house. You needn't leave this process to guesswork: Your Lowe's Flooring Consultant can arrange for you to take home samples of all the candidates.

Don't forget that you'll need to purchase one or more thresholds to cover the transition between the bathroom and adjoining floors. There are two types to consider. A flush threshold sits at the same height as the new flooring, and must be cut precisely to meet it. An on-top threshold spans the joint between the new surface and the one it abuts. Thresholds come in a variety of materials, including metal, hardwood, and natural stone. A metal-strip threshold accommodates different flooring heights and is easiest to install, but it may not be the best-looking choice unless your floor abuts carpeting. Wood and stone thresholds are available either premade or by special order. A wood threshold must be properly sealed.

Following are the most common options for flooring material in the bathroom.

VINYL It's not hard to see why vinyl has outsold all other types of bathroom flooring for years: It's attractively priced, durable, skid resistant, easy on the feet, and a breeze to maintain. It's also available in a vast selection of colors and

styles. Stability and water resistance make it suitable for any location, even a below-grade bathroom. With proper surface preparation, it can be installed over any standard underlayment, including concrete, ceramic tile, wood, or existing vinyl flooring.

Vinyl is available in sheets or tiles. Sheet vinyl comes in 6- or 12-foot-wide rolls. Vinyl tiles are manufactured in 12- or 18-inch squares. Both are secured to the underlayment with adhesive.

There are two types of vinyl flooring: printed and inlaid. Printed vinyl is produced much like a magazine page, with the pattern photographically applied. Inlaid vinyl has color granules embedded into the vinyl sheet. Though considerably more expensive, inlaid vinyl has a richer finish and lasts much longer.

The biggest determinant of durability

Suggestive of tumbled stone, designer-quality high-performance 16-inch-by-16-inch resilient tile flooring offers great looks on a budget.

LOWE'S QUICK TIP

To determine how many square yards of flooring you'll need, just enter your room dimensions into the Flooring Calculator at Lowes.com.

bathroom flooring

The beauty of limestone is achieved economically with this glazed ceramic tile, complemented by accent strips that look hand-carved.

to have sheet vinyl installed by a professional unless you're a careful, experienced, and motivated do-it-yourselfer. Vinyl tiles, especially self-adhesive ones, are relatively simple to install (see page 198 of the Do-It-Yourself Guide).

Vinyl can be torn, burned, dented, and scratched. Damaged sheet flooring may require complete replacement. Vinyl tiles are easy to replace if they're damaged, but they can collect moisture between seams and may work loose over time even if they're kept dry. Proper installation and careful use can prevent problems.

CERAMIC TILE For elegance at an affordable price, nothing beats tile. Its classic, handcrafted look adapts to any decor, and there are so many configurations and finishes to choose from that the design possibilities are practically endless. Properly installed, a tile floor will be watertight and easy to maintain. With minimal care it will last for decades.

Ceramic floor tile is commonly manufactured in 4- to 12-inch squares, although sizes can range from 1 inch to 24 inches, and other shapes such as octagonal and hexagonal are available. Larger tiles make for quicker installation and fewer hard-to-clean grout lines. Smaller tiles with more grout lines offer extra traction, and they often come premounted on 12-inch-square sheets of paper or mesh for easier installation. You can expand your design options by combining tiles of different shapes and sizes.

Ceramic tiles come in glazed and unglazed versions. Glazing adds stain resistance and allows for the use of brighter colors. Three different finishes are available in glazed tiles: glossy, matte, and textured. For a bathroom floor, slip-resistant matte or textured glazes are safest. Unglazed tiles, also called quarry tiles, have a rugged, naturally skidproof surface because they're unfinished. They are water resistant, but must be sealed to resist stains. Color choices are limited to

(and price) in vinyl flooring is the surface coating, or "wear layer." A vinyl no-wax wear layer is sufficient for areas with light traffic and minimal exposure to dirt. A urethane coating resists scuffs, scratches, and the vicissitudes of normal to heavy foot traffic. Enhanced urethane, which has the highest-quality surface coating, holds up under the heaviest use and maintains its luster longer than other coatings. If you're choosing between two vinyls with the same coating, check the thickness: In general a thicker floor is a better floor. Along with significant variations in quality, you'll find a wide range of prices. Vinyl tiles can cost as little as 60 cents a foot, while the most expensive inlaid sheet vinyl can cost 10 times that much.

Vinyl must be installed over a perfectly smooth underlayment, since even tiny bumps and dirt specks may eventually show through the vinyl's surface. It's best natural earth-tone shades, and the look is definitely rustic.

Porcelain tile, made by firing fine white clay at extremely high temperatures, is amazingly tough and stain resistant. It is sold in just about any color and texture, including types that resemble marble, travertine, and even terra-cotta.

The tile you buy should have a rating that matches the use it's going to get. Some tiles are rated for indoor or outdoor use only; others can be used in either application. Other ratings describe a tile's relative hardness, durability, and porosity. A tile's porosity rating, which measures how much water it absorbs, is most crucial for a bathroom installation.

Costs for ceramic tile generally range from inexpensive to moderate, although handmade tiles can be quite pricey, and specialty products such as tempered glass tiles can cost $30 a square foot or more. Installation is labor-intensive and thus tends to be expensive. Tile requires a very stable subsurface, which often means an added expense for building up the subfloor. You can cut costs by installing your own ceramic-tile floor, but you'll need a tile cutter and plenty of time and patience (see page 200). To save money on materials, use inexpensive field tile for the bulk of your installation, sprinkling in a few high-end pieces as accents. To add visual interest, arrange plain tiles on the diagonal or use colored grout.

Ceramic tile's chief disadvantage is its tendency to harbor dirt and bacteria in grout spaces. You can mitigate this by using an epoxy grout (a darker shade will be easier to care for) and keeping grout spaces thin and regular. Tile can also be cold underfoot. If you're building an addition or opening up your subfloor, consider installing radiant floor heating.

STONE A stone floor is the epitome of luxury in a bathroom. Natural stone surfaces such as marble, granite, limestone, and slate are classics for traditional-style baths, and their smooth, clean look adapts just as readily to a contemporary design. Tough and water resistant, they need little upkeep to last for generations.

Stone can be cut into tiles or used in its natural shape, known as flagstone. Tiles are preferable for bathroom flooring because they can be butted tightly together; a flagstone installation will require wider grout joints that can attract stains and mildew. Stone tiles usually come in 12-inch squares that must be cut with a wet saw. They are affixed to the underlayment with a thinset base.

Stone may have a glossy surface, or it may be "honed" for a subtler, softer look. Honed surfaces are less slippery underfoot. All stone except granite is porous and will absorb dirt and stains, so it's

Decorative embossed tiles beautifully accent the natural tones of this ceramic tile, used in several sizes on the floor, counter, and walls.

bathroom flooring

absolutely essential to apply an efficient sealer at least once a year. Some stones, such as marble, are easily scratched; be sure to test them before buying.

A stone floor can be a budget-buster, but it needn't be: Some stone tiles cost no more than high-quality sheet vinyl. Installation is costly if done professionally and challenging for a do-it-yourselfer. The weight of the material requires a very solid, well-supported base, which may mean that you'll have to spend time or money building up your subfloor. Affix your flooring with white thinset, because some stone tiles are translucent.

The most common hardwood flooring is made from oak, but other species are available in a range of finishes. Some woods are harder than others, meaning that they're more resistant to scrapes and dents. If your bathroom gets a lot of traffic, you may want to use a very hard material such as maple or bamboo. However, a wood's hardness doesn't determine whether it will cup or gap (reclaimed wood is actually the most stable because it has already endured countless fluctuations in temperature and humidity).

There are two types of hardwood flooring: Engineered flooring is laminated in a manner similar to plywood, then finished with a hardwood veneer; solid flooring is cut from solid pieces of wood and milled to standard specifications. Both are available as strips (3 inches wide or less) and planks (more than 3 inches wide). Wood tiles, called parquet flooring, are also available. Parquet is normally manufactured in a 12-by-12-inch square consisting of narrow strips of wood.

No matter what wood you use, the key is to keep moisture from getting between the boards by sealing the surface of the floor well.

LAMINATE Laminate flooring can mimic the look of traditional wood floors as well as tile, stone, and other materials. The surface of laminate flooring is a highly

BELOW: Natural limestone makes a stunning statement on the floor of this elegant bathroom.

HARDWOOD A hardwood floor has a warm, rich appearance that looks inviting in a bathroom. Though wood's aversion to water makes it a nontraditional choice for the bathroom, it can work beautifully as long as it is properly installed and thoroughly sealed.

RIGHT: Defined lines and dark tones characteristic of slate are mimicked by this durable high-pressure laminate floor.

detailed photographic image covered with an extremely tough plastic wear layer. Because it's durable and easy to clean, laminate works well in a bathroom. However, moisture can ruin the floor. Follow the manufacturer's instructions to prevent dampness from seeping between or below the planks.

Laminate floors are floating floors, meaning that they aren't attached to the subfloor. Instead, planks are fastened to one another, either with an adhesive or by locking together. Laminate flooring can be installed on all grades, including the basement. With proper preparation, installation is possible over concrete, vinyl, tile, and even some carpet.

CARPET Carpet is quiet, warm underfoot, and available in all kinds of styles and colors. Because of its tendency to hold moisture, it's best suited to dry areas of multiuse bathrooms and master suites.

Carpeting comes in a variety of fabrics and weaves. For the bath, choose short-pile, unsculptured materials. Stain-resistant fibers and finishes are making carpet a more practical option than ever before. The most effective treatments are added as part of the manufacturing process; finishes applied later are not as long-lasting. Nylon and other synthetic carpets hold up best in moist areas. Natural fibers such as sisal and seagrass are good choices as well, since they actually prefer a slightly damp environment.

Even if you're a careful housekeeper, keep carpeting out of splash zones. Near the tub or toilet, it's apt to attract mildew, stains, and microorganisms.

CORK Soft and warm underfoot, cork makes a very comfortable flooring surface for a bathroom. It's also antimicrobial and resistant to mold and mildew. However, you'll need to protect it from water.

Use only cork tiles (not a floating floor) for a bathroom installation, and caulk the perimeter of the room prior to

installing the molding or the baseboard. This will prevent any spills from damaging the subfloor or walls. Though cork floors are often prefinished, it's a good idea to apply at least one extra coat of polyurethane after installation. Maintain the surface by sealing it on a yearly basis. Cleanup requires only sweeping and damp-mopping. A well-maintained cork floor will last for decades.

LINOLEUM Linoleum is an old-fashioned natural flooring that's enjoyed a revival in recent years. Warm underfoot and beautiful to behold, linoleum is bacteria resistant, biodegradable, and one of the longest-lasting floor coverings you can buy. Because colors are mixed in during manufacturing, the pattern runs all the way through the linoleum, so your floor will look good until it's been worn down to the jute backing.

Linoleum is made from harvestable raw materials, including linseed oil, wood flour, and pine resin. It's manufactured as 12-inch tiles or sheets, and comes in a wide range of rich colors, with patterns ranging from marbled to mock-crocodile. Unlike sheet vinyl, linoleum should be polished periodically. Installation can be tricky, especially for those accustomed to working with sheet vinyl. If you're hiring a professional, make sure it's someone who has worked with linoleum before.

The super-durable fibers of this nylon carpet protect it from soil, stains, and moisture while controlling static electricity.

wall treatments

THE WALL COVERINGS AND TREATMENTS in your bathroom are more than just a fashion statement. The wall covering you select should be able to withstand moisture, heat, and scrubbing. Paint, wallpaper, ceramic tile, stone and even wood paneling are all viable options, provided you use types and techniques that are appropriate for bathroom walls.

paint

No decorative element gives you more bang for your buck than paint. It's the cheapest wall covering you can find, and the most versatile. It comes in any color you can dream of, and produces a panoply of finishes that mimic anything from marble to mahogany. Its tough surface adheres tenaciously and cleans up easily. For just a few dollars, you can repair it when it gets damaged or replace it when you want a new look.

BELOW AND RIGHT: **Complementary shades of blue 100 percent acrylic paint give this sun-bleached bathroom a seaside color scheme.**

Paint consists of pigments that supply color, binders that hold the pigments together, and liquid that disperses the pigments. When you apply paint to the wall, the liquid evaporates (cures), leaving the solid pigments and binders behind. The label on a can of paint will tell you the percentage of solids in the product; a higher percentage usually means you're buying a thicker paint that will provide better coverage.

Paint may be either latex or oil/alkyd, depending on whether water or mineral spirits are used to disperse the pigments. Oil/alkyd-based paint clings to the wall a little better than latex (water-based) paint, and it provides a smoother, more durable finish. However, oil/alkyd is more difficult to apply, takes longer to dry, and brushes must be cleaned with turpentine or paint thinner. Latex paints, especially low-toxic

versions, are much safer for the environment and the painter, and new 100 percent acrylic formulations perform as well as oil/alkyd-based products. Cleanup requires only soap and water. Latex paint tends to show brush strokes unless it's applied in thin layers. It dries fast, so you'll have to work quickly in hot weather.

Sheen describes paint's light-reflecting qualities. Types include gloss, semi-gloss, satin, and flat. Some manufacturers also make eggshell, which has a sheen between flat and satin. Gloss is the toughest, most-scrubbable finish, but its high sheen will magnify imperfections in the surface you're painting (be sure the surfaces are flat and smooth). Lower-luster semi-gloss and satin finishes have enough moisture resistance for the bathroom but will be a little harder to clean. Avoid flat paint, which will soak up moisture and stains. If you're covering newly installed drywall or bare wood, be sure to apply a primer first. Choose a latex primer if you plan to use latex paint, and an oil-based primer if you're using oil/alkyd paint.

wallpaper

Wallpaper is a powerful decorating tool that can bring out the best in your bathroom. By taking advantage of pattern and texture, you can use wallpaper to hide a room's flaws or enhance its assets, making it appear wider, narrower, roomier, more intimate, or just more striking. The only caveat is that the moisture in a bathroom will soon get the better of any wallpaper that's not suited to the job. When you're shopping for wallpaper, make sure you choose one that's moisture resistant, and don't compromise on quality.

An infrequently used guest bath is the perfect place for wallpaper because it remains dry most of the time. A powder room is another good spot, since the lack of a tub or shower means there's no steam to affect the wallpaper's adhesion. Most quality wallpapers, if applied properly, will work even in a bath that gets steamy

on occasion, especially if the room is well ventilated (see page 127).

Wallpaper comes in a variety of materials, including textiles, grasscloth, foil, and vinyl. Vinyl wallpaper is moisture resistant and easy to clean, which makes it the preferred choice for bathrooms. Metallic or foil wall coverings look striking and stay put in moist conditions, but they are difficult to install, and they will continue to cling to the wall when you want to remove them. Embossed paper with a glossy finish will repel modest amounts of moisture and will stand up to occasional wiping, which makes it worth considering for a bathroom that gets occasional use. Wallpapers made of natural fibers will soak up stains, and some (particularly grasscloth) are extremely difficult to remove.

Wallpaper may be prepasted, self-

A natural shade of green brings balance and beauty to this bathroom with sedated hues that encourage relaxation.

wall treatments

adhesive, or nonpasted. Prepasted versions are manufactured with a coating of adhesive that you can activate with water. Self-adhesive wallpaper comes with a backing that you peel off before sticking the paper in place. Nonpasted (sometimes called "dryback") wallpaper must be coated with adhesive before it can be hung. Most prepasted and self-adhesive wallpaper is either strippable or peelable, an important consideration unless you won't remodel again for a few decades or you won't mind scraping dime-size bits of soggy paper from your wall when you want to make a change.

It's important to consider how the pattern of your wallpaper will look in your bathroom. Horizontal patterns will make the room seem wider, but you should avoid them if your ceiling and walls are not perfectly square. A vertical pattern will make the ceiling seem higher, but it, too, will call attention to crooked or sloping walls. For a room that isn't square, choose a pattern that repeats diagonally across the strip of wallpaper.

Residential wallpaper is manufactured in American rolls, which have approximately 35 square feet of wallpaper per roll, and European rolls, which have approximately 28 square feet per roll. Allow for at least 15 percent waste, more if you're using a large repeating pattern. Be sure to check the pattern number and the run number of each roll of wallpaper you buy. Run numbers, which indicate a particular dye lot, should be identical so there's no variation in color.

other options

Durable, easily cleaned, and classy, ceramic tile makes an ideal covering for bathroom walls. It withstands wet conditions, and lasts for decades with little upkeep. It comes in so many colors, textures and configurations that you'll never run out of decorating options.

The old-fashioned wood paneling known as wainscoting can add extra character to a country- or traditional-style bath without adding much to the bottom line. As a bonus, it will protect a new wall or conceal any imperfections in an old wall.

Natural stone materials such as granite, marble, limestone, and travertine make an opulent-looking wall treatment in a bathroom. You can have stone slabs fabricated to serve as wall panels, a very expensive option, or you can use stone tile, a less costly choice that offers many of the advantages of ceramic tile.

Solid-surface material is a practical, attractive choice for shower walls, and you can have it fabricated to fit any bathroom wall. In fact, just about any material that's suitable for a bathroom countertop can be used as a wall covering.

lighting & ventilation

NO MATTER WHAT THE SCALE OF YOUR remodel, it pays to invest some time in developing a well-planned lighting scheme. Lighting has an especially dramatic impact in a bathroom, and it makes a relatively minor dent in the budget. The right light fixtures, carefully placed, can help transform your bathroom into a retreat that's safe as well as stylish.

Artificial lighting is divided into three categories. Ambient lighting provides general illumination. Task lighting focuses on a particular area where extra light is needed for activities such as shaving or makeup application. Accent lighting is used to highlight a specific detail such as a work of art or an attractive architectural feature. Any well-designed living area, including the bathroom, should have a combination of all three types. The room should also be lit from various levels: below, mid-range, and overhead. By "layering" a variety of light sources at different heights, you can reduce glare and create flattering, even illumination.

Adequate ambient light is the foundation of a bathroom lighting plan. In a small bathroom, light fixtures above or beside the mirror may provide enough illumination for the entire space. In a larger bath, ambient lighting is usually positioned overhead. Recessed lighting is a popular choice because it has a low profile that's perfect for small spaces (if you choose recessed lights, be sure to angle them so that the light bounces off the walls and ceiling to minimize glare and

shadows). Ceiling fixtures also provide good general illumination.

Overhead lighting can and should be supplemented with other sources. Cove and soffit fixtures create a wash of ambient light that can make a small room

Sconce lights with chrome bases and domed glass diffusers are a contemporary take on the age-old candle.

lighting & ventilation

ABOVE: **Fitted with up to 12 bulbs, vanity strips provide excellent illumination at a mirror.**
BELOW: **Surface-mount fixtures come in a wide variety of designs; these glass domes are two popular models.**

seem bigger. Low-voltage fixtures in a toe kick supply diffused illumination from below and double as nightlights. Wall-mounted fixtures fill in gaps at midrange.

Task lighting should be concentrated around the mirror—an area where adequate illumination is critical (and becomes even more important as time goes on, for at the age of 55 we need twice as much light to see as we did in our 20s). Light should shine on the person, not the glass, and it should come from both sides of the mirror as well as from above: An overhead fixture by itself will cast shadows on your face while you're grooming. To be most effective, wall-mounted fixtures should be located at eye level and positioned to shed light equally on both sides of the face. Theatrical-style strip lights also work well if installed alongside and atop the mirror. Choose frosted bulbs instead of clear ones to help minimize shadows. To double the effect of any fixture, attach it directly to the mirror so the light is also reflected (be sure the fixture you choose

can be installed flush with the glass so its unfinished backside won't be visible in the mirror).

Task lighting may be desirable in other areas for reasons of convenience or safety. A light in the shower or over the tub can help prevent accidents and make it easier to shave, for example (be sure that fixtures over the bathtub or shower are UL-rated for use in those areas). Overhead track fixtures can illuminate dressing-room shelves or light the way in and out of the shower. Recessed light fixtures can be aimed to provide concentrated down-lighting for accents or tasks.

Other choices include pendants, undercabinet strip lighting, wall sconces, or even table lamps (but be sure not to place them near water).

When you're shopping for fixtures to fit your lighting scheme, look for models that will blend with the style of your bathroom. Decorative fixtures are available in a huge array of finishes that can be coordinated with faucets, pulls, and hardware. Nickel, brass, and chrome are the most popular. Chrome is durable, affordable, and coordinates well with mirrors. Old-fashioned materials such as iron and vintage glass have a warmer appearance. If you want track or pendant lighting, be sure your ceiling height is adequate. For glare-free light, choose fixtures with translucent lenses, and avoid colored lenses—they won't supply the clear light that's needed in a bathroom. Dimmer switches will further reduce glare and allow you to change the mood of the bathroom by controlling light levels. They also save energy, extend lamp life, and eliminate the need for nightlights.

Bulb selection is as important as choosing and placing fixtures. The three prima-

Like the vanity strip, this type of multilamp lighting provides even illumination but comes in a variety of styles to complement a non-modern decor.

ry types of lighting are incandescent, halogen, and fluorescent. Incandescent bulbs are the least expensive, but they use a lot of energy and burn out quickly. Low-voltage versions, which are a little more expensive, work beautifully for accent lighting. Halogen lighting provides full-spectrum light, making it the best choice for illuminating the bathroom mirror (it produces the most realistic colors for applying makeup). Halogen bulbs are more expensive than incandescent ones, but they last longer. Because they generate quite a bit of heat, they can be used only in fixtures appropriate for them and should not be placed too near the ceiling. Fluorescent lighting—once disfavored for bathroom use because it caused skin to appear yellowish—is now available in a wide spectrum of hues that look more natural. Fluorescent bulbs are big energy savers, and they're ideal for hard-to-reach fixtures because they seldom need replacing. All bulbs will last longer in fixtures that light down.

Make it a point to read packaging and instructions when you're purchasing bathroom lighting. Fixtures should be UL-approved and suitable for use in damp areas. Check with local building inspectors about electrical codes: There may be restrictions on where various lighting fixtures can be placed.

ventilation

Most building codes require ventilation—a window or a fan—in bathrooms. Unless it's adequately ventilated, your beautiful new bathroom will soon be plagued by mold and mildew, ceiling drips, peeling paint, and a host of other moisture-related problems. Open widows, doors, and skylights will help reduce bathroom dampness, but to ensure sufficient ventilation you need an exhaust fan.

To be effective, a bathroom fan must be powerful enough to replace the air in the room at least eight times an hour. Fans are sized according to how many cubic

feet of air they can move in a minute at a given pressure, expressed as cubic feet per minute (CFM). To determine what CFM rating your fan should have, multiply the total cubic footage of the room by 8, then divide by 60. If the room's CFM requirement falls between fan ratings, choose a fan with the larger rating.

For bathrooms larger than 100 square feet, the Home Ventilation Institute recommends a ventilation rate based on the number and type of fixtures present. Toilets, showers, and tubs require 50 CFM each; a whirlpool tub requires 100 (for more on sizing a vent fan, visit the Home Ventilating Institute's website at www.hvi.org). You can install separate fans over the tub, shower, and toilet, or use one larger fan that will pull air through the entire room. Steam showers should always have a separate fan.

But even the brawniest fan will be ineffective unless it is ducted to the exterior of the house through the roof, an exterior wall, a soffit, or an eave. Many fan manufacturers make special fittings for this purpose. It is all-important to follow manufacturer's instructions regarding ducting. Use the proper size duct pipe, and minimize bends.

It's not enough simply to exhaust steam from the bathroom during a shower. Residual moisture from wet towels, rugs, and washcloths will keep the humidity high long after the bath is finished. To remove this moisture, outfit your fan with a humidistat that will automatically turn the fan off when humidity has dropped to an acceptable level. Alternatively, you can run the fan for at least 20 minutes after you use the shower or tub (an automatic timer can do the job for you), or set up a portable dehumidifier.

To boost the performance of your exhaust fan, install a return-air grille above the bathroom door. Since steam rises, the high vent will allow humidity levels to equalize between rooms even with the door closed.

Powerful yet quiet bath fans quickly eliminate humidity and odors from the bathroom. They're available in many styles and shapes; light/fan combinations perform double duty as a ceiling light fixture.

windows, skylights &

BELOW: **In this bathroom, an operable skylight combines with a wall of windows to fill the space with light.** BELOW RIGHT: **This airy bath feels like part of the patio, thanks to its doors and windows.**

IN A BATHROOM, WINDOWS HAVE A big job to do. They must admit natural light while protecting privacy. They may be called upon to improve ventilation yet keep out cold and heat. In addition, they need to survive in moist conditions and complement the surrounding decor.

Doors, too, face special challenges in the bathroom. Often they have to work with a cramped space or a high-traffic hallway. They get heavily used, so they need to be sturdy. They're expected to dampen noise, so they have to be solid. Because they remain closed a good deal of the time, they have to look attractive from both inside and out.

Windows and doors are major architectural features that can represent a major portion of your remodeling budget. Be sure to choose products that will function efficiently and enhance your comfort for years to come.

windows

Windows come in many shapes, sizes, and styles; for a bathroom it's best to select an operable window that can be opened to promote ventilation.

Operable windows come in many configurations. The classic choice for a traditional bath is the double-hung style, which has two sashes that slide up and down. European-style "tilt-turn" windows are double-hung windows with a top sash that can be removed, rotated, or tilted for cleaning. Casement windows, which are

doors

LEFT: **A round-top transom window provides a focal point for this tub alcove.** BELOW: **In this generous bathroom, an expanse of casement windows captures a panoramic view.**

easy to fully open, have hinged sashes that swing in or out with the turn of a crank. Horizontal sliders, more contemporary in appearance, usually have two side-by-side sashes, one or both of which can be slid open. An awning window is essentially a top-hinged casement that tilts out at the bottom.

Windows can be made from wood, aluminum, vinyl, or a combination of these materials. Historically, windows have been constructed from wood, which is still the most popular option. Because it doesn't conduct cold or promote condensation as other materials can, it's a good choice for the bathroom. However, wood will swell, warp, and rot when exposed to water, so it must be well sealed.

Aluminum windows usually come with an anodized finish that doesn't need painting. Many versions have extruded vinyl and foam insulation, which reduces heat loss and condensation. You may not be able to paint aluminum window frames, and they will deteriorate quickly in coastal areas due to the salty air.

Vinyl windows, the least expensive option, are made from rigid, impact-resistant polyvinyl chloride (PVC). High-quality vinyl windows are resistant to heat loss and condensation, but inexpensive ones have a tendency to distort when exposed to extremes of cold and heat. Vinyl windows can't be painted, and colors may fade over time.

Clad-wood windows are made from wood that's been covered with a tough

jacket of extruded aluminum or vinyl. The cladding, available in a few stock colors, keeps the exterior sash and frame virtually maintenance-free. Vinyl cladding is colored throughout, so scratches are inconspicuous. Aluminum cladding, though it will show scratches, is tougher, and comes in a wider variety of colors.

Windows can cause significant energy loss if they're not well chosen, leading to chilly bathroom temperatures and higher heating bills. To minimize this problem, choose glazing (window panes) with excellent insulating ability. The two ratings to check are R-value and U-value. R-value indicates how well a glass prevents heat and cold from entering the house. U-value is a more comprehensive indicator that tells you how much heat or cold flows through the entire window, including the frame. A high R-value indicates better insulating ability; a low U-value indicates greater energy-efficiency.

Most windows today have two or three panes of glass sealed together; the space between the panes is filled with an insulating layer of air, or with argon gas, which is an even better insulator. If the unit isn't properly sealed, condensation can occur between the panes, causing permanent cloudiness. It's a good idea to look for windows that have a strong warranty so you'll have recourse if the seal fails and condensation occurs.

Low-emissivity (low-E) glazing is layered with a special film that screens out some unwanted solar rays but still lets in light. Low-E coatings can help keep your bathroom warm on cold days and cool on hot days, and they protect bathroom surfaces (and bathers) from ultraviolet rays.

skylights

Skylights provide up to 30 percent more natural light than vertical windows, and they can make a small space seem bigger. In a bathroom with limited wall space, a skylight may be your only means of bringing in more daylight.

Like windows, skylights are either stationary or operable. Fixed skylights provide illumination only. Ventilating models can be opened and closed by means of a

A recessed, slanted skylight follows the roofline to illuminate this upstairs bathroom.

hand crank, a wall switch, a remote control, or a high-tech automatic temperature sensor. When it's open, a ventilating skylight can create an updraft that will draw hot, steamy air from the bathroom.

Old-fashioned skylights were simply a single thickness of glass in a frame, but today they come with low-E and tinted coatings to control heat transmission and UV radiation. Skylights are rated for their thermal efficiency in the same way windows are, so you can compare R-values and U-values for different models (see above). As an alternative to tinted glass, which darkens the room, you can get shades or blinds for your skylight. Ventilating skylights can be equipped with screens to keep out insects.

When a full-size skylight is too big for your bathroom, you can get almost as much light from a tubular skylight. Just 10 to 18 inches in diameter, tubular skylights consist of a clear dome over a reflective shaft that ends at the ceiling with a sealed diffuser. The system provides an enormous amount of light for its small size, and it's sealed to minimize heat gain and loss.

Light-block shades turn day into night. Made of fabric with exterior aluminum coating, they're very energy efficient.

Pleated shades distribute soft filtered light, reducing glare and the fading effects of UV light on furnishings.

Venetian blinds offer optimal control over the direction and concentration of light, and are easy to fit.

bathroom doors

Installing a pocket door, or re-hanging a hinged door so it opens out, can expand the comfort zone in a small bathroom, where every inch counts.

There are three basic types of doors: hollow-core, solid-core, and solid wood.

Hollow-core doors are a popular option for many do-it-yourselfers. They are priced for the budget-conscious and are light and easy to handle. They come with either smooth or molded surfaces. Smooth doors have a stain-grade veneer of lauan, oak, or birch, so you can stain or paint it to match your decor. The surface of a typical molded door is made of hardboard molded into a multipanel design. The most popular style is the traditional six-panel, but other classic styles are also available. Hardboard is a durable material that resists shrinking and swelling. The paintable surface has a wood texture, providing the look of wood-paneled doors for a budget price.

Solid-core interior doors look and feel like solid wood doors, but they feature a wood-fiber core. They offer greater sound-quieting properties than hollow-core doors, and they can withstand rougher treatment. While these are not "fire doors," their solid core offers extra fire protection, since it burns through slower than a hollow door. The solid-core door offers the style and properties of a wood door without the cost.

Solid wood doors can be stained or painted for a rich finish. Solid wood has natural sound-deadening qualities. The properties that give wood its character may determine if these doors are an option in your home. They are very heavy, and you may need an extra hand to install them, but the weight gives solid wood doors a stable feel. Wood swells and shrinks over time and with humidity changes, so more precision is required during installation. Oak and white pine doors are very popular, but other types of wood are available through special order.

POCKET DOORS

Pocket doors recede into the wall instead of swinging out, saving 8 to 10 square feet of floor space—highly valuable in tight spaces such as powder rooms. They are practical, too—they pull shut for privacy, yet tuck away for complete openness—and add dramatic style.

Pocket doors have typically been mass-produced cheapies or attractive but pricey custom-made products. But now you can choose pocket doors that combine aesthetics, affordability, and reliability all in one door.

TYPES AVAILABLE

- Because you simply attach standard doors (minus knobs) to pocket-door track systems, the majority of interior doors measuring 1⅛–1¾ inches thick and weighing up to 125 pounds will work. Although you once needed to have decorative-glass or specialty-panel doors custom-made, many styles are now offered as stock items.
- Some hardware kits can even accommodate doors weighing as much as 200 pounds.

FEATURES TO CONSIDER

- Buy a high-quality hardware kit (track system) that will evenly carry your door's weight and has rollers that won't jump the track. Make sure your door style fits within the kit's size requirements, too.
- If you need privacy in the rooms on either side of the pocket doors, choose a solid-wood or frosted-glass door and outfit it with a lock system available from the hardware manufacturer.
- The early phase of a remodeling project is the best time to decide you want pocket doors because they are best installed when your walls are being framed.

window treatments

IN THE BATHROOM, THE MOST IMPOR-
tant function of window coverings is to
provide privacy. But window treatments
also control light, dampen noise, and
keep out cold and heat. In addition, they
help define your bathroom's style.

You can begin the process of selecting
window coverings by deciding what

would look best in your bathroom. Fabric
window treatments such as curtains and
Roman shades can have a welcome, soft-
ening effect in the bath, where shiny, hard
surfaces predominate. Blinds and shades
look sleek, and can be drawn up out of
sight so that other decorative details can
play a starring role. Shutters have a crisp,
architectural appearance that complements cabinetry and moldings.

ABOVE: **Energy-efficient
fabric blinds let in light
and maintain privacy;
draping fabric swags
further soften the look.**
RIGHT: **Aluminum hori-
zontal blinds offer
outstanding control.**

You can choose from any of the following window-covering styles, as long as
you select appropriate materials:

CURTAINS & DRAPERIES These are most
often semi-opaque, meaning that only
shadows can be seen from outside the
window. When paired with linings that
add opacity and durability, they offer
complete privacy. Tiers, which cover only
the lower half of the window, are a great
choice for the bath if windows are high
enough. They permit plenty of light to
enter while still protecting privacy. Sheer
and semi-sheer curtains will allow visibility from outside. If you love the gossamer
look of sheers, you can combine them
with opaque window treatments such as
shades or blinds.

FABRIC & ROLLER SHADES Most roller
shades are made of opaque vinyl or fabric, while Roman, balloon, and other fabric shades generally are lined.

PLEATED & CELLULAR SHADES In non-sheer fabrics, these combine privacy with decorating flexibility. Many styles can be ordered with a "top down" feature, so the upper portion of the shade can be lowered to let in light. Cellular shades are champion insulators because their honeycomb design traps a protective layer of air.

BLINDS Made of wood, aluminum, vinyl, or synthetic wood lookalikes, blinds provide privacy. Wood may warp and aluminum may rust over time unless your bathroom is well ventilated (see page 127 for more on ventilation). Faux wood and vinyl blinds will tolerate bathroom dampness, but budget versions may fall apart, so shop carefully.

SHUTTERS Shutters may be made from vinyl and sold off the shelf, or they may be custom-crafted from wood, like fine furniture for your windows. Both high-end and budget versions of shutters provide adequate privacy. The same caveat applies to wood shutters as to wood blinds: Avoid them unless your bathroom has excellent ventilation.

PRIVACY WINDOW FILM A thin sheet of translucent plastic that is applied directly to the window glass, privacy window film can protect your solitude without darkening the bathroom. Frosted film is the best choice for a bathroom because other types provide only daytime privacy. You can also buy window film designed to reduce glare, reflect heat, or provide insulation, but they, too, will be completely transparent at night.

Before you shop for coverings, measure each of your bathroom windows separately, using a steel measuring tape. Do not assume that all are the same size. If your window coverings will be mounted inside the window frame, record the narrowest width and the longest length for every window. For gap-free coverage on an outside mount, record the maximum width. If you're on a budget, choose stock window coverings. If you're ordering custom window coverings, ask Lowe's about special options, including insulating liners and cordless operation.

ABOVE LEFT: **Moisture-resistant faux-wood blinds can be tilted by optional remote control.** BELOW: **A curved head rail hides these overlapped fabric shades when they're raised.**

project workbook

IF YOU'RE UPDATING YOUR BATHROOM BY REPLACING A SINK OR INSTALLING a new light/fan fixture, you can probably move right on to the Do-It-Yourself Guide that begins on page 156. But if your bathroom remodel is more involved—calling for several new fixtures, flooring, cabinetry, and structural changes—the job will present plenty of challenges. This chapter is designed to give you all the information you need to meet those challenges.

This workbook will help you plan every aspect of your bathroom remodel, from distilling and prioritizing your dreams to working with installers and contractors. Information, questions, and checklists will guide you through the entire process, helping you create a bathroom that is perfectly suited to your family's needs and lifestyle.

You'll begin by considering your family's habits, preferences, and priorities, particularly focusing on those of the people who will use the bathroom most. During this phase, you'll make the major decisions about the type of fixtures and cabinets that will be appropriate for the bathroom. These decisions will give you the basis for creating a personalized design.

Then you'll be ready to take inventory of everything you need to get your project done, including assessing how much of the work you're prepared to do yourself. To help with this part of the process, you'll find valuable information about securing financing, obtaining permits, drafting contracts, working with Lowe's, and hiring and managing other professionals.

Whether you're giving the powder room a facelift or building an entire in-home spa, this workbook will assist in making your remodel as efficient, affordable, and painless as possible. Follow it as you would a road map, or simply peruse it for points of interest. The answers you find along this journey will help you create a beautiful, practical bathroom that's perfect for your needs.

developing a plan

ONCE YOU'VE DECIDED TO REMODEL your bathroom, how do you begin? Your practical side (not to mention various contractors and well-meaning relatives) may tell you to start by determining how much you can spend. But that's a bit like planning a vacation by consulting your checkbook instead of a guidebook. So begin your remodel by envisioning your ideal bathroom, down to the last detail. Though you may have to make a few compromises along the way, you're much likelier to end up on target if you know where you want to go.

A sketch or simple floor plan of your existing bathroom can be very useful during planning. A T-square, scale ruler, and triangle can help you draw one accurately.

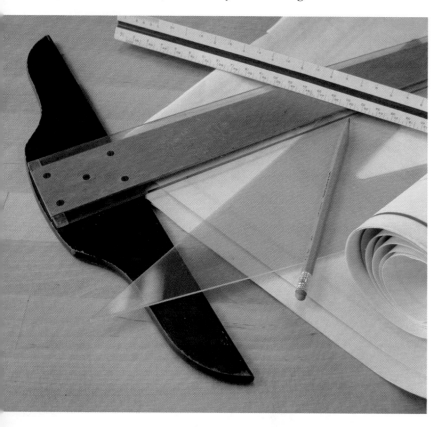

focus on **preferences**

Your first task is to decide exactly how you'd like your new bathroom to look. A good place to start is the chapter that begins on page 10—it's packed with pictures of remodels and makeovers that may spark your imagination. After you've gathered a few ideas, expand your search. Visit the Lowe's website (www.lowes.com) for design and product ideas. Clip pictures from magazines and make a scrapbook of your bathroom favorites. Check out remodels that your friends have done and look for features that appeal to you. Attend a home show. Take a neighborhood home tour. As you go about this process, pay close attention to your responses and note whether you are consistently attracted to certain motifs, materials, or features. In particular, focus on the following key design elements:

COLORS Are you drawn to warm, cheerful hues or to cool, soothing ones? Keep in mind that light tones and monochromatic color schemes can make a room seem more spacious, while dark colors can close in a space. You'll be living with many of your color choices for a long time to come, so think carefully about whether you'll still want fuchsia tiles in the shower five years from now.

SURFACES Do you want the sleek opulence of natural stone? Does the traditional look of ceramic tile appeal to you? Choose rough textures to create an informal mood, smooth surfaces for elegance. Imagine how all your surfaces—from cabinets to flooring to vanity tops—will work together.

SPACE Do you consider small rooms cozy or confining? Would an extravagantly large bathroom delight you, or would you rather put the space to another use? Have you always longed for a dressing room, an exercise room, or some other bathroom add-on? Would you like a defined area for the toilet or vanity, or would you prefer an open plan? The size of your bathroom should determine the scale of your fixtures, cabinets, and other large elements. To visually expand the room, include plenty of windows, avoid extra-large appurtenances, and keep your overall design simple.

STYLE Is your taste traditional or contemporary? Do you want your bathroom to have a casual look or a polished one? What does the rest of your house look like? You don't need to slavishly mimic existing color schemes or themes, but you should probably think twice before putting a Baroque bathroom in your Craftsman bungalow. In short, avoid mixing dramatically different styles.

be practical

Next you'll need to consider what kind of bathroom will really work for your family. Gather your household members together and discuss the following issues. Also, fill out the questionnaire on page 140, which will help your Plumbing Sales Specialist (or your contractor, if you hire one) to advise you.

USE How many people will be using the bathroom? Will you need two sinks, extra counter space, or a separate area for the toilet? Do you need to create access from two bedrooms? Do you typically shower and run, or do you love to linger in a candlelit bath? Is a whirlpool tub on your

must-have list? A separate stall shower? A vanity table? Do you dream of a bathroom with a walk-in closet or an indoor atrium? Visit a Lowe's store to discuss your needs with a Plumbing Sales Specialist, or take advantage of the suggestions you'll find on the Lowe's website. When you're ready to choose cabinets, fixtures, and fittings, the Buyer's Guide that begins on page 76 can help you figure out what products and features are best suited to your family's needs.

WEAR AND TEAR Are you vigilant about keeping the bathroom free of hair-dye spills and heaps of wet towels, or would you be better off with flooring and countertops that won't stain and warp? Is your two-year-old (or your teenager) likely to assault the faucet handle? Consult the Buyer's Guide on page 76 to research the practicality and durability of products you're considering.

EASE OF CLEANUP Be sure to evaluate ease of care and upkeep when considering various materials. The Buyer's Guide (page 76) contains information about cleaning and maintenance.

ACCESS AND SAFETY Will anyone using your bathroom need, or find it helpful to have, grab bars, a shower seat, or extra room to maneuver a wheelchair? How about a very short person, or a very tall one, who might need special heights or clearances? Also consider safety. It can be wise to take this opportunity to install temperature-controlled faucets, slip-resistant surfaces, and other safety features.

SPACE AND STORAGE Do you have ample space for the exercise area or sauna you crave? Can you be satisfied making changes within your existing space, or will it be necessary to knock down walls to get the bathroom you want? How much storage will you need? Which items will require cabinet space and which can be

developing a plan

stored in drawers? Do you want a laundry hamper or chute? A linen closet? A vanity?

DISRUPTION Discuss how much upheaval you can tolerate. Of course, the bigger your project, the more it will encroach on your life. Is this your only bathroom? If you decide to add square footage, can you contend with the noise, dust, and inconvenience that attend a major remodel? (See page 152 for information on controlling disruption.)

identify your **priorities**

You want your remodel to be fast, easy, inexpensive, and high quality. Often the best you can hope for is three out of the four. That's why it's crucial to identify

what's really important to you. To do this, make a list that includes the following:

- What you absolutely must replace. If your toilet is rust-stained and won't flush properly, deciding whether or not to buy a new one is a no-brainer.

- What you absolutely can't bear to keep. Your vinyl flooring may still be serviceable, but if it's just not your style, give it the heave-ho.

- What you absolutely can't live without. Will you kick yourself if you give up that whirlpool tub or those handmade tiles? Leave a little room in the budget for the luxuries you really want.

A base map of your bathroom's existing dimensions is critical for developing a new design and planning bath improvements.

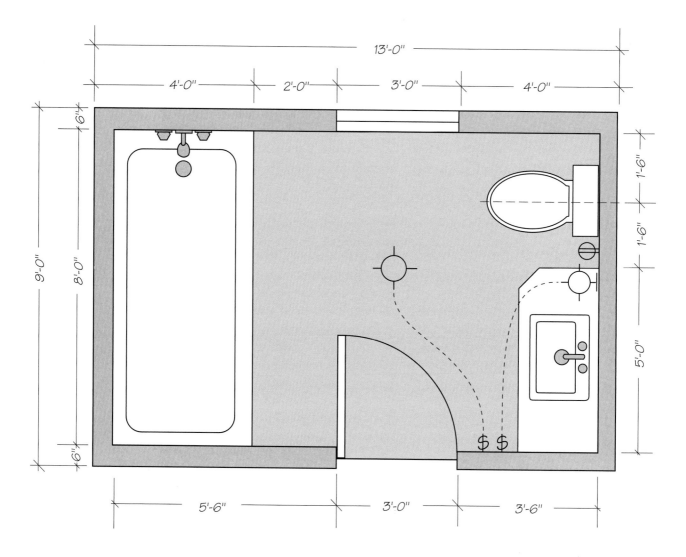

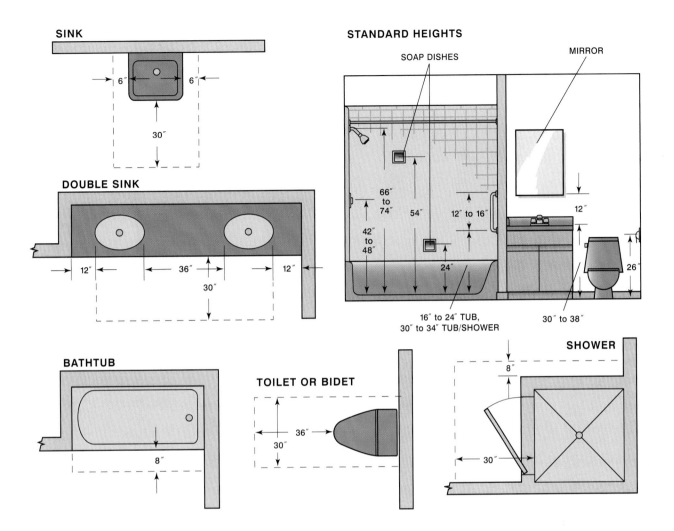

SINK

6″   6″

30″

DOUBLE SINK

12″   36″   12″

30″

STANDARD HEIGHTS

SOAP DISHES

MIRROR

66″ to 74″

54″   12″ to 16″

42″ to 48″

12″

24″

26″

16″ to 24″ TUB,
30″ to 34″ TUB/SHOWER

30″ to 38″

BATHTUB

8″

TOILET OR BIDET

36″

30″

SHOWER

8″

30″

take existing measurements

Using a steel tape measure, take your bathroom's basic measurements and jot them down on a rough sketch (working on graph paper is easiest). Be sure to include the entire length of each wall, as well as the space between doorways, windows, and major bathroom elements, including sink, tub and/or shower, and toilet. Note which direction your door or doors swing, where electrical fixtures, outlets, and plumbing are located, and anything else that might ultimately have impact on your new bathroom design.

When you're ready to redesign your space, you can adapt this base map (see opposite) to create a new floor plan. Just leave intact the parts of your existing bathroom you intend to keep, and add the features you want. An Installed Sales Coordinator at Lowe's can help you plan installations of new products and fixtures.

If you choose to design your new bathroom without using professional services, start by sketching in the bathtub and/or shower on your map; make sure you've allowed plenty of room for a shower door to swing open if you've opted for one, and for bathers to get in and out of the tub or shower stall. Next, position the sink (or sinks), allowing space for easy access and traffic patterns. Place the toilet away from the tub, preferably where it will not be visible when the bathroom door is open. Finally, check your layout for efficient heights and clearances. The illustrations above show the industry guidelines for these dimensions. Also check building codes to see what clearances are specified by law in your area.

A bathroom's layout and design should pay close attention to standard clearances and heights to ensure safe and convenient use of fixtures.

LOWE'S BATHROOM QUESTIONNAIRE

Fill out the form below as thoughtfully and as thoroughly as you can with the household members who will be the primary users of your bathroom remodel or new bathroom. Your responses will help you and your Lowe's Plumbing Sales Specialist tailor your new bath to your lifestyle, family, wish list, and budget.

BATHROOM USE

This bathroom is to be:

☐ Remodeled   ☐ New construction

What kind of bath will it be?

☐ Master   ☐ Shared

☐ Children's   ☐ Half

The existing bath

Tub

Color_____

Size_____

Material_____

Shower

Color_____

Size_____

Material_____

Sink

Color_____

Size_____

Material_____

No. of faucet holes_____

Toilet

Color_____

Size_____

Material_____

Tub and shower faucet size (hole spread)_____

Vanity

Dimensions_____

Stained or painted?_____

Vanity top

Material_____

Color_____

Special storage needs:

☐ Cleaning supplies

☐ Curling iron

☐ Electric razor

☐ Hair dryer

☐ Hot rollers

☐ Linens

☐ Makeup

☐ Paper supplies

☐ Toiletries

☐ Towels

EXISTING BATHROOM FEATURES

Cabinetry	☐ Keep	☐ Change
Colors	☐ Keep	☐ Change
Counter space and surface material	☐ Keep	☐ Change
Door(s)	☐ Keep	☐ Change
Finish materials	☐ Keep	☐ Change
Flooring	☐ Keep	☐ Change
Hardware	☐ Keep	☐ Change
Layout	☐ Keep	☐ Change
Lighting	☐ Keep	☐ Change
Storage space	☐ Keep	☐ Change
Windows	☐ Keep	☐ Change

NEW FIXTURES

Shower faucet

Color/Material _____ Dimensions_____

Manufacturer_____ Model #_____

Sink

Color/Material _____ Dimensions_____

Manufacturer_____ Model #_____

Sink faucet

Color/Material _____ Dimensions_____

Manufacturer_____ Model #_____

Toilet

Color/Material _____ Dimensions_____

Manufacturer_____ Model #_____

Toilet seat

Color/Material _____ Dimensions_____

Manufacturer_____ Model #_____

Tub

Color/Material _____ Dimensions_____

Manufacturer_____ Model #_____

Tub faucet

Color/Material _____ Dimensions_____

Manufacturer_____ Model #_____

financial issues

THOUGH A MINOR BATHROOM UPDATE might be relatively easy to handle within normal family finances, a major remodel may involve some financial planning. It's wise to begin by focusing on remodeling economics—that is, determining whether you'll get a reasonable return on your investment when you sell your home—particularly if you may sell within the next few years. Read on for suggestions about setting a budget, obtaining financing, and controlling costs.

return on investment

You can't put a price on increased enjoyment of a new bathroom, but it's smart to pay attention to potential return on your investment when determining the extent of work it will entail. Provided that you intend to stay in your house for at least a year, you can often recoup a substantial portion of your remodeling costs when you sell, and in some markets you may even get back more than you spent. No matter where you live, a bathroom remodel is one of the most profitable home improvements you can make (second only to a minor kitchen remodel). But be cautious: You're unlikely to be rewarded for creating a bathroom that's far grander than the others on your block, since buyers usually won't pay more than a 10 to 15 percent premium for a house that's better than its neighbors. Nor will you profit by outfitting a modest home with a bathroom more suitable for the Taj Mahal. Of course, if you

know you'll be staying in your house for a long time, or you simply want a new bathroom regardless of whether the next buyer will value it, then you can forge ahead and forget about this part of the planning process.

anticipating costs

Bathroom remodels can run from a few hundred dollars to a hundred thousand or more, depending on the extent and quality of the work. Simple installations of plumbing fixtures, cabinets, and flooring can be quite affordable. Structural changes, on the other hand, can be expensive. If you plan to build an addition, move a load-bearing wall, alter a ceiling or roofline, restructure a floor, or install windows or skylights, you'll need to beef up your budget accordingly. If you're able to work within the space you

Simple improvements such as painting, laying a new floor, and replacing a toilet and sink usually offer a solid return on investment when you sell your home in the future.

financial issues

have, just new cabinets can account for one-third the cost of a new bathroom. Plumbing and electrical changes can also cause the bottom line to balloon. On the other hand, you can keep costs down by maintaining locations of existing fixtures.

Revisit your planning questionnaire (page 140) and your floor plan, and consult the Buyer's Guide on page 76 to see what features you'd like. Then make a trip to Lowe's (or to www.lowes.com) to compare your options; have your base map with specific measurements handy so you can accurately estimate your cost for everything from fixtures to flooring.

managing costs

If you come up with a heart-stopping estimate for your bathroom remodel, review your biggest expenses and consider whether you can reduce the overall scale of the work. If you're planning structural changes to an existing bathroom, can you work with your existing space instead? Can you keep a window size the same to avoid reframing a wall? Can you achieve much of what you want by simply replacing old fixtures or by doing cosmetic improvements?

If you're building a new bathroom, placing it near the kitchen or an existing bathroom can streamline the work because the existing water supply, drain lines, and vent stack can sometimes be used. Or you might arrange fixtures against only one wall to eliminate the cost of additional plumbing lines.

You can also make significant cuts to the bottom line by revising your plans for cabinets, fixtures, and other major design elements. Perhaps you can choose stock cabinets instead of custom-built ones or select mid-price fixtures instead of high-end models. Check out less-expensive materials for countertops and flooring; creative use of vinyl flooring, laminates, and other moderately priced surfaces can result in a fabulous look.

Since labor can account for a signifi-cant part of a bathroom remodel, you can save a lot of money by doing work yourself. Even an amateur handyperson can handle many simple jobs, but be realistic about your time, tools, and skills. Take a look at the Do-It-Yourself Guide that begins on page 156 for step-by-step instructions on how to perform basic remodeling tasks. Lowe's can also be an excellent source of advice.

methods of financing

Let's say your new bathroom's estimated cost exceeds your bank balance by a factor of 10. Be careful about incurring credit-card debt because interest rates are high, and you can't deduct the interest from your taxes. Instead, check into getting a loan. Several options for borrowing money are available, and most are tax-deductible. Here are the basic choices:

REFINANCE You can get a new mortgage on your house, taking a larger loan than you had before to pay for your improvements. You'll start over with a new interest rate and, in most cases, you'll pay points and closing costs just as you would on any mortgage.

HOME-EQUITY LOAN You can borrow against the equity in your house—that is, the difference between what your house is worth and the amount you owe on it. You may pay a higher interest rate than you would on a refinance, but closing costs are generally lower. Ask the bank or lender to compare up-front expenses and monthly payments.

HOME-IMPROVEMENT LOAN If you have little or no equity in your home, this may be your only option. There are several types of home-improvement loans, all secured with the future value of your house. Interest rates are almost always higher than those for a refinance. As with home-equity loans and mortgages, the interest is tax-deductible.

hiring professionals

LOWE'S CAN TAKE YOU FROM YOUR magazine clippings and rough design to a completely installed new bathroom. Step by step, Lowe's professionals will work with you in turning your plans into a reality, including specifying and pricing the materials and fixtures you'll need. A Lowe's Installed Sales Coordinator will be happy to quote you a price for removing and replacing such things as flooring, cabinets, lavatory and pedestal sinks, sink faucets, toilets, and lighting.

Another option is to hire any of several independent professionals such as an architect, general contractor, or designer.

Lowe's services

When you shop at Lowe's, you can work with a Plumbing Sales Specialist to outfit your bathroom plan and to arrange for installation services. All of the work is done by professionals. Most important, Lowe's guarantees the results. Just tell your sales specialist which items you'd like to have installed, and pay for the items and installation services at the same time. Shortly after your purchase, you will be contacted by one of Lowe's professional installers to schedule your installation at a time that's convenient for you. To find out more about how Lowe's professional installers can help with your bathroom remodel, visit your Lowe's store.

independent pros

Following is a closer look at some of the independent professionals who might

play a part in your remodel, particularly if the improvements will involve considerable new construction.

BATH DESIGNERS Bath designers can help you come up with an entire bathroom plan, not to mention tell you about the latest trends and techniques. If you decide to hire an independent designer outside of Lowe's, ask about credentials, talk to satisfied former clients, and view examples of previous work. Also see "Interior Designers" on page 144.

If your new bathroom will call for exquisite workmanship or expensive materials—such as this stunning bathtub and its surrounds—it pays to hire professionals to do the work unless you have considerable experience.

hiring professionals

GENERAL CONTRACTORS General contractors specialize in construction, but the job description can vary. Some contractors handle all the work themselves, while others do nothing but schedule and supervise subcontractors. Some offer design services, while others require you to provide a professional-quality plan.

SUBCONTRACTORS Subcontractors such as plumbers, electricians, and carpenters specialize in a particular aspect of construction. You can act as your own general contractor and hire subcontractors yourself. With this type of arrangement, you can choose to do some or none of the work yourself.

ARCHITECTS Architects can handle a remodel from start to finish: They can design a functional, attractive space; get bids from general contractors; and supervise the actual work. They're also able to make calculations for structural changes; other professionals aren't allowed to make such changes unless a state-licensed engineer designs the structure and signs the working drawings.

Improvements that involve structural work, new wiring, or plumbing often call for the talents of a contractor. Significant structural changes may require an architect or engineer.

INTERIOR DESIGNERS Interior designers focus on designing, decorating, and furnishing a room, including space planning, figuring layouts, and specifying materials. Many will also supervise the work. They have access to materials and products not available at the retail level.

do you **need a pro?**

Deciding whether to hire a professional is one of the most crucial choices you'll make when planning your new bathroom. If you have the time and the determination, you can do quite a bit of the work yourself—even if you don't have much experience. Many remodeling tasks are relatively simple and straightforward. And if you do choose to fly solo, Lowe's has experts on staff to advise you, and stores offer classes to give you hands-on experience in everything from setting tile to painting.

However, if you're thinking of performing as your own contractor, be aware that this is a real job. It involves ordering your own materials and keeping detailed records of purchases and deliveries, as well as finding qualified subcontractors who will work at reasonable prices, learning about local building codes and obtaining permits, dealing with inspectors, and handling insurance and possibly even payroll taxes.

Before stepping into this role, consider the following:

Do you have the skills? Even neophytes can tackle many of the jobs outlined in the Do-It-Yourself Guide that begins on page 156. However, unless you're a very experienced and skilled do-it-yourselfer, you may be better off leaving more-complex tasks in the hands of professionals.

How visible will the results be? The more prominent the improvement, the more you'll need professional-quality work. Save skill development for places not readily seen.

Can you work safely? Make sure you

won't be endangering yourself or your family when you work with electricity, gas, and tools—or with heavy loads or on precarious perches.

Do you have the time? Doing your own home improvement, presumably on a part-time basis, can extend the duration of a project considerably; if speed is a priority, call in a pro. If you do decide to go it alone, keep in mind that most people underestimate how long a job will take. To be on the safe side, double the amount of time you think you'll need. You'll also want to build in extra time to

repair any mistakes. Don't neglect putting a value on your time, and consider whether the money you'll save is really worth the time you'll spend.

Do you have the tools? A major bathroom remodel can call for a wide variety of tools. You can buy new tools or rent specialized equipment. But remember that buying and renting tools will add to the bottom line. If the cost of obtaining tools adds significantly to your budget, a professional's bid might seem more appealing—unless you see this as a chance to expand your tool collection.

FINDING A QUALIFIED PROFESSIONAL

A skilled professional can be an invaluable asset when remodeling your bathroom. It's important to find someone with a proven track record and a personality you find palatable. Here are some steps you can take to find a professional who meets your needs:

- Visit Lowe's. Your Lowe's store offers a wide variety of remodeling and installation services, and all work is guaranteed to meet Lowe's specifications.

- Get recommendations from several sources. If you have friends who have recently remodeled, ask them to refer you to any professionals they found reliable. If you already know and respect a professional, ask him or her to recommend specialists in other aspects of bathroom remodeling.

- After you have gathered several names, interview those professionals with experience working on projects like yours (for a big job, talk to at least three).

- Request written, itemized bids that include a breakdown of time, materials costs, and labor rates. Ask if the work will be guaranteed and, if so, for how long.

- Pay attention to your gut reaction. You're beginning a relationship with someone who will be in your house every day. If you feel uncomfortable, even if you can't pinpoint the reason, keep looking.

- Request names of former clients from the professionals you are considering. When you contact them, ask these important questions: 1) Was the project completed as promised and on time? 2) Was the person prompt, reliable, and tidy? 3) Did (s)he deal effectively with other professionals on the job? 4) Was (s)he easy to work with and pleasant to have around?

- Ask to see some completed projects. Most design and construction professionals can supply photographs, and some are even willing to arrange for you to visit former clients' homes.

- Ask about logistics. Will the person you're hiring do the work, supervise others, or some of both? Will (s)he be working on other jobs simultaneous with yours? How long will the job take? When will work begin?

- Make sure your candidates have appropriate credentials. General contractors should be licensed and bonded; if your state has a contractors' board, it can provide information about current licensees and any complaints lodged against them. Architects are licensed by the state as well. Many professionals also belong to trade organizations such as the American Institute of Architects, the National Kitchen & Bath Association, or the American Society of Interior Designers.

- Talk about money. Will you receive a firm bid, or will you be expected to pay for the person's time and the cost of materials? If the deal is for time and materials, will the bid include a "not to exceed" figure?

- Inquire after each person's status with the Better Business Bureau (703-276-0100 or www.bbb.org).

agreements

WHEN LOWE'S PROVIDES INSTALLATION services for your bathroom remodeling project, product quality and satisfactory installation are guaranteed. Your Plumbing Sales Specialist will help you fill out a simple agreement that outlines the work to be performed. However, if you choose to work with independent professionals, a number of important points should be outlined in a written agreement. This will help prevent misunderstandings and disagreements and serve as a backup if a dispute should arise.

what it should include

A contract is a legal agreement that obligates the people who sign it to perform specific acts. Note the word "specific." Make sure any contract you sign spells out exactly what you expect from any professional you hire. Here are some elements you should include:

- Start and finish dates. You may want to include the phrase "time is of the essence," which can give you added leverage if a construction or other delay leads to a dispute.

- The right to settle disputes by arbitration. In the event of a dispute, this may be speedier and less costly than a court proceeding.

- A warranty of at least a year on all work and materials. Some states require a contractor to warranty his or her work for at least five years (10 years for hidden problems).

- A payment schedule. When working with Lowe's, you pay for goods and services upfront, then count on Lowe's long-standing reputation to oversee quality workmanship. But when working with an independent building contractor, no matter how highly recommended, it is important to provide continual incentives for completing the work (and to protect yourself from a contractor who might take off with your money) by phasing payments. Check with your state contractor's board for recommended practices. If speed is important, you may want to include a late-penalty clause and/or a bonus for early completion.

- Detailed job and materials descriptions. Be sure of your choices before you draw up the contract, then spell them out. If you want flooring made of a certain type of marble tile, put it in writing. Be sure that contractual allowances will cover the cabinets, fixtures, and materials you want; a $29 faucet may look better on a bid than it will in your bathroom.

- A waiver of subcontractor liens. In some states, subcontractors can place a lien on your property if the general contractor fails to pay them. To protect yourself from this, specify that final payment will not be made until the contractor gives you an unconditional release of these rights from all subcontractors and suppliers who provided services and/or materials.

- If amendments, or "change orders," are made along the way, be sure both parties initial them.

avoiding **conflicts**

A contract will help you establish productive relationships with the professionals you hire, but it's no guarantee your remodel will go smoothly. A piece of paper cannot substitute for basic courtesy and common sense.

Use this book to educate yourself about the fundamentals of remodeling so you'll understand what the professional is proposing and why.

Before you sign a contract, study it carefully to verify that you and the professional have the same understanding of the work to be done. Double-check your research to be sure that contractual price caps will cover the costs of the bathroom elements you want.

When professionals arrive at the job site, respect their skills. It's fine to ask questions and keep tabs on the progress of your project, but don't niggle, pester, or hover.

By all means be polite, but do speak up promptly if you have a concern. It will be much more difficult to make a change once the job is finished.

HANDLING INDEPENDENT CONTRACTOR PROBLEMS

If you're unhappy with the way your contractor is handling your remodel, your first step should be simply to express your concerns face to face. Most contractors will make every effort to ensure that you're satisfied with their work. Should you reach an impasse, an architect, designer, or other professional who knows your project may be able to help broker an agreement. If such personal approaches don't work, you can take one or more of the following actions, but by all means start with the least-drastic measure:

1. Send a certified letter outlining the contract requirements you consider to be unfulfilled and stipulate a reasonable time frame for compliance. Sometimes this is enough to inspire action.

2. File a complaint with the Better Business Bureau (BBB) at 703-276-0100 or www.bbb.org. The BBB will forward your complaint to the contractor, who may reconsider your requests in order to avoid an unfavorable BBB report.

3. Contact the local or state board that licenses contractors. Contractors have a strong incentive to maintain a clean record with the licensing board, since some boards have the power to levy a fine or even revoke a license in cases of serious negligence or incompetence.

4. If both parties agree, try to resolve the dispute informally through a mediator. The BBB and many local organizations offer mediation services to help businesses and consumers work out mutually agreeable solutions without going to court.

5. Present your case before an impartial arbitrator. More formal than mediation, but generally less costly and time-consuming than litigation, arbitration gives both parties the opportunity to present evidence in a joint hearing. The arbitrator's decision is usually binding. You can arrange arbitration through the Better Business Bureau, or through the American Arbitration Association (www.adr.org).

6. If you're seeking minimal damages (the amount allowed varies from state to state but is usually no more than a few thousand dollars), bring your case to small claims court. You won't need an attorney, and court costs are usually modest.

7. If you're suing for a large amount of money, you can file a civil suit, but this option has definite drawbacks: The case may drag on for months or even years, and your costs can exceed any award you may receive. Remember that if you have fired a contractor who has essentially done the work as agreed, you are the one who will be found to have breached the contract. Make every effort when drawing up a contract to be explicit about the work to be done.

codes & permits

PERMITS FROM YOUR CITY OR COUNTY building department are required before you can begin certain types of projects. Though changing a toilet, faucet, floor covering, or similar item doesn't call for a building permit, changes to your home's structure, plumbing system, or electrical wiring do. You may also need to submit detailed drawings of the changes you plan to make before you begin. During construction, the building department will send inspectors at several points to verify that the work has been done satisfactorily (usually, it is up to you to schedule the inspections).

A general contractor or architect, if you have one, can handle all of this for you. Each is familiar with local building codes and can be enormously helpful in getting plans approved, obtaining any variances, and making sure that you pass inspections.

things to do

For those who decide to act as their own general contractor, here is a to-do list:

- Check with your building department before you get too far into planning an addition. Local codes usually specify how far from the property lines a house must be. If your addition will be too close, you may need a variance, or you may be prohibited from building it at all.

- Find out whether you'll need to submit your plans for approval.

- Ask the building department to give you printed information about the ordinances that apply to your remodel and the various types of permits you'll need, if any.

- If you're a diehard do-it-yourselfer, be aware that in some regions only certified electricians or plumbers are legally allowed to install or upgrade wiring and pipes.

- Prepare for inspections. Read pertinent sections of the building code so you'll know exactly what the inspector will be looking for (see "Inspections" on the following page). If you've hired

Because installing a whirlpool tub involves electrical wiring and plumbing, this job almost always requires permits and inspections.

buyer could demand that you bring the work up to code.

inspections

When you obtain a permit for your bathroom remodel, your building department can tell you what inspections you'll need and when they should be done. Some types of work require more than one inspection. For example, electrical work is inspected when circuits are roughed in, again when changes to the electrical service are completed, and finally when all electrical devices have been installed, grounded, and energized. Inspectors will look for the following when they visit your worksite:

LEFT: **It's important to keep a set of approved building plans and inspection records on site so building officials can refer to them.**

subcontractors, ask them to be present when their work is inspected.

why get a **permit?**

Permits exist to protect homeowners. If a professional suggests you don't need one for major work, check with the building department yourself: You probably do, and it's to your advantage to get one. In fact, this suggestion is usually a red flag that your contractor is trying to cut corners to the detriment of the work. In most cases, you'll pay a fee based on the value of the project (so don't overestimate it or you'll pay more).

A permit ensures oversight of the work. The scrutiny of an inspector can guard against mistakes and shoddy workmanship and give you assurance that the work adheres to building codes. You'll sleep better knowing that your project meets safety standards for materials and construction techniques.

Obtaining a permit will also help you avoid headaches in the future. If building officials discover you've done work without a permit, you could be required to dismantle your remodel and start all over again. If you sell your house, you may be legally obligated to disclose that you've remodeled without a permit, and the

- A copy of the building permit, posted where it can be seen easily.

- A record of all inspections that have been completed and signed off.

- Proof that equipment such as wiring and pipes was installed by certified professionals, if such requirements exist in your area.

- Compliance with local codes, including safety and zoning issues. Obtain copies of all relevant ordinances from your building department.

WHEN DO YOU NEED A PERMIT?

You probably need a permit if you plan to . . .
- Change the footprint of your house by adding a new bathroom or enlarging an existing one
- Move a load-bearing wall
- Alter the roofline
- Create a new door or window opening
- Move a sink
- Replace plumbing fixtures

But not if you plan to . . .
- Install new floor coverings
- Replace doors or windows without altering the structure
- Change a countertop
- Replace a faucet

project management

YOU CAN COUNT ON YOUR REMODEL causing a certain amount of upheaval in your household, especially if you only have one bathroom. But there are some simple steps you can take to make the ordeal a bit more bearable.

First, plan the progress of your remodel carefully: You don't want to pour the foundation for an addition that violates local ordinances, or gut your bathroom only to find that the fixtures you ordered haven't come in yet. The timeline here

planning
ONE MONTH OR MORE

■ Purchase and arrange for delivery of any new cabinets and fixtures.

■ Inspect items as they arrive. Have the delivery person wait until you're certain no returns will be necessary. If

your purchase came from Lowe's, promptly report any problems; Lowe's stands behind every product it sells.

■ Rent a refuse bin for demolition debris, if necessary. You may also want a portable toilet for construction workers (and for your family, if you're temporarily decommissioning your only bathroom).

■ Meet with your contractor, job-site supervisor, architect, or designer to discuss exactly what needs to be done. Finalize a daily schedule, set ground rules for the project, and arrange communication logistics with those overseeing the work.

■ Pack up and move your personal belongings from the work area.

demolition
TWO DAYS

■ Set up refuse bin and portable toilet.

■ Cover doorways with heavy sheets of clear plastic to contain dust and debris. Seal well, and check frequently.

■ Shut off electricity, then water.

■ Remove fixtures, starting with the tub.

■ Remove countertop.

■ Remove cabinets.

■ Handle any structural demolition.

will help you complete your project as quickly as possible with a minimum of costly interruptions. If you hire subcontractors, follow the schedule at right ("Sequencing Trades") to make sure that each one is available at the right point in the process.

During construction, a few precautions will mitigate the effects of remodeling on your family and your possessions.

before you begin . . .

Get a permit from your building department. Do not proceed until your project gets the go-ahead or you could be wasting time and money. Order custom-made items such as windows, doors, and granite or marble countertops.

SEQUENCING TRADES

If you're acting as your own general contractor, one of your most important tasks is scheduling the subcontractors. Errors in scheduling can be costly and inconvenient. Ask your subcontractors how long each step of your project will take, then schedule their arrival in the following order:

1. Rough carpenter
2. Heating and air-conditioning contractor
3. Plumber (rough plumbing)
4. Electrician (rough wiring)
5. Drywall contractor
6. Cabinetmaker or installer
7. Countertop installer
8. Plumber (finish work)
9. Electrician (finish work)
10. Flooring contractor
11. Finish carpenter
12. Painter

construction
THREE TO SIX WEEKS

- Lay the foundation, frame the walls and floor, install doors and windows, if necessary.

- Install ductwork for heating and air-conditioning.

- Update electrical service if necessary, and install rough wiring for outlets, switches, and lighting.

- Route water lines and drainage pipes.

- Install roofing and siding, if necessary.

- Hang and finish drywall.

finishing
TWO TO THREE WEEKS

- Install fixtures.

- Install cabinets, including doors and hardware.

- Install countertops; be sure to allow for any delay in receiving specially ordered materials.

- Install lighting, switches, and receptacles.

- Install underlayment for flooring, if needed. If you've chosen sheet vinyl, install it at this point and cover it carefully to protect it during ongoing construction.

- Install flooring. Allow a day or so for resilient or laminate flooring, two days for hardwood, up to a week for tile or stone, depending on the size of the room.

- Paint and install trim.

- Prime and paint walls.

- Install electrical and lighting cover plates and trims.

controlling disruption

Even when everything goes smoothly, a bathroom remodel can be trying; when things go wrong, it can be downright traumatic, especially if remaining bathroom facilities are inadequate. You can minimize irritations and prevent calamities by taking a few simple precautions:

- Plan carefully. It's a grievous and unnecessary inconvenience to live with a hole in an exterior wall while you're waiting for the out-of-stock window you should have ordered earlier.

- Time the work to avoid inclement weather (you'll have to contend with muddy footprints and wind whistling through your missing exterior wall) and major holidays (not much work will get done). Also avoid giving yourself an inflexible deadline: If you're planning to have guests around Christmastime, for example, you're pushing your luck to start your remodel the day after Thanksgiving.

- Don't go on vacation. Even if you have a general contractor, you'll need to make decisions and keep an eye on the progress of your remodel.

- Do arrange to be out of the house for a short time when it's noisy, workers are working with substances that give off fumes, or other activities are taking place that you'd rather not be around.

- Get phone numbers for all the key people working on your project, and ask the general contractor for a home number and/or cell phone number. Make sure that every tradesperson knows how to reach you. If you don't have a cell phone, seriously consider getting one.

- Establish and post a set of house rules regarding the use of phones and rooms, keeping pets indoors or out, and similar issues.

- Seal interior doorways with plastic sheeting and duct tape to keep out dust, especially when sanding drywall.

- Be mindful of home security. Remember that you may have hordes of strangers in your house. Be careful about giving out keys and burglar-alarm codes. Don't leave valuables in plain sight or unattended.

remodeling safely

Above all, you want to emerge from your remodel in one piece—with both your house and your family intact. Remodeling can be a dangerous business, and careless work habits can cause disasters and even death. Talk with your insurance agent about your homeowner's policy and any

During construction, be prepared for plenty of dust! Keep lots of duct tape and plastic sheeting on hand for sealing up doorways to isolate work areas.

additional coverage you should maintain during your remodel. If you're using a contractor, be sure (s)he is covered for liability and workers' compensation. If you're doing the work yourself, watch for potential hazards whenever you're on the job, and take these precautions:

- Keep the work area well lit and uncluttered. Plan your setup before you begin. Clean up as you go, removing debris that might cause uncertain footing. Don't leave tools lying about.

- Wear appropriate clothing, including long pants and sturdy shoes or workboots, as well as safety gear (see items at right). Never wear loose-fitting clothing that could catch in a tool's mechanism; tie back long hair.

- When using anything that emits fumes, keep the area very well ventilated.

- Use only power tools that are double-insulated or grounded. In a damp area, be sure you plug into an outlet protected by a ground fault circuit interrupter (GFCI or GFI; see page 189).

- Keep tools in good working order. Make sure that blades and bits are sharp and safety devices such as guards are undamaged.

- Don't lift loads that are too heavy, and do bend at the knees when you pick up large items. Work with a partner when you need help, but avoid working with another person in tight places where you could injure each other.

- Don't work when you're tired. You're most likely to be injured while cutting "just one more" tile or 2 by 4.

- Shut off power in the service panel before beginning any electrical work or opening up walls where wiring may be

present. Be sure you know which circuit breakers control which circuits. Use a neon tester to double-check that the circuit is off. Working with electricity is one of the riskiest jobs you can undertake. If you're not sure you can handle a task, call in a professional.

SAFETY GLASSES Protect your eyes when using power tools or tools that involve striking an object (a hammer and chisel, for example).

HARD HAT Wear one if you will be working with a partner in a cramped space or if falling objects could hit you.

EAR PROTECTORS Use these when you will be working with machinery that is noisy.

RESPIRATOR OR DUST MASK Be sure that a respirator or dust mask is approved for filtering the pollutants you are handling, including dust, fibers, and harmful vapors.

GLOVES Choose leather to protect your hands from scratches and splinters, rubber when handling any caustic chemicals.

bathroom safety

This thoughtfully designed bathroom incorporates many safety and universal-design features, including ample access, grab bars, rounded corners, and resilient flooring.

NEARLY A QUARTER OF ALL HOME accidents occur in the bathroom. Slippery surfaces, tight spaces, and the proximity of water to electricity make the bathroom one of the most dangerous places in the house. Given this, it's wise to consider safety issues when planning a remodel or new construction. These sorts of improvements are appreciated by everyone, from young children to guests. A few preventive measures can make your new bathroom safer for everyone.

planning for safety

Be sure all work is done according to building codes and inspected by building officials. This will ensure that all gas lines, plumbing, wiring, and general con-

struction meet minimum safety standards.

Incorporate safety solutions into your bathroom layout. Provide ample room for exiting the tub and/or shower. Make sure an open cabinet door won't suddenly become a hazardous obstacle.

Keep safety in mind when you're shopping for fixtures and materials. Select slip-resistant surfaces whenever possible, and make sure any rugs or bath mats have a nonskid backing. Consider materials (such as resilient flooring) that will soften the impact should someone fall. To avoid bumps and bruises, round all countertop edges and use flush cabinet pulls (or at least types without sharp edges). Use shatterproof material for shower doors.

To prevent scalds, lower the temperature on your water heater and install a temperature-limiting mixing valve or a pressure-balancing valve. Or, consider purchasing a programmable faucet that allows you to set the water temperature you want.

Make sure you can access the bathroom in case of an emergency. Every bathroom should have a second access or a way to get its locked door open from outside the room.

Take special care when mounting objects to walls: Position sharp-ended towel bars out of eye-level range—and choose only rounded towel bars for children's bathrooms. Be sure cabinets are anchored firmly to wall studs. Install grab bars, preferably with plywood reinforcing and bracing between wall studs.

Plan for safe storage of all dangerous implements and toxic chemicals. If young children are in the household, equip cabinets with safety latches or locks.

Give careful consideration to proper lighting to minimize the kinds of accidents that can occur when visibility is impaired. Window shades or blinds can help control glare, and dimmer switches make it possible to vary light levels.

Make sure you have enough properly grounded outlets—and that they are well

Childproof latches on doors make cabinets safer when children are in the house.

Vinyl flooring is slip resistant and resilient underfoot.

A thermostatic temperature control valve protects against scalds and water-temperature dips during showers.

located—to eliminate the need for extension cords. Place outlets out of reach of the tub or shower, and make sure they are protected by ground fault circuit interrupters (see page 189).

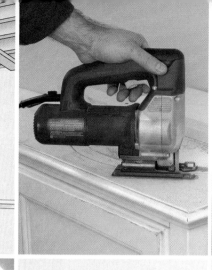

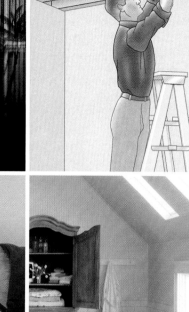

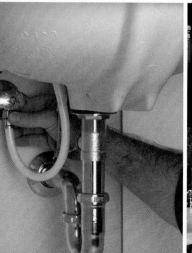

do-it-yourself guide

IF YOU ARE HANDY, OR ENJOY LEARNING NEW BUILDING SKILLS, YOU ARE PROBABLY considering taking on some, if not all, of your bathroom remodeling work. There are many good reasons to do at least some of the work yourself, the primary one being your budget. Without a doubt, you can save money, or put that savings toward more expensive materials or little extras. You may learn new skills, or hone the ones you have. You can assure quality control over the project. And then, of course, there is the pleasure of the process itself, and the satisfaction and pride that come from improving your home yourself.

As you consider the benefits, you will also want to take a long, hard look at the realities. Honestly evaluate your skill level before undertaking more-complex tasks, since mistakes can end up costing you more than if you had hired a professional from the start. And take stock of your tools, making sure you have—or can buy or rent—the necessary ones for the job. Also figure out how long it will take you to complete a project, particularly if you have a full-time job. Nothing is worse to live with than a half-done remodeling project, particularly when it is a bathroom. For more about deciding whether or not to do the work yourself, see page 144.

If you do choose to do some of the work yourself, one or more of the projects presented in this section may be perfect for you and your skill level. Four "families" of projects are presented on the following pages: Wall & Ceiling Improvements, Plumbing Improvements, Electrical Improvements, and Surface & Cabinet Improvements. These projects cover basic work that many, if not most, do-it-yourselfers with some experience should be able to take on comfortably. Each project is clearly presented with step-by-step photographs or illustrations and explanatory text to walk you through the job. Be sure to take note of any warnings set in red in the margins, and take advantage of Lowe's Quick Tips to speed you through the work.

tools & materials

WHETHER YOU'RE COMPLETELY RE-modeling your bathroom or simply repainting the walls, it's important to take stock of the tools and materials you'll need before you begin.

Shown here and on page 160 is a basic collection of tools that can be used for a broad range of bathroom improvements. They are used repeatedly throughout the step-by-step projects on the pages that follow. More-specialized tools are discussed in each project's instructions—you can rent or buy these as you choose.

layout tools

COMBINATION SQUARE A square helps you draw straight lines across lumber to be cut; it also helps you check angles on assembled pieces of a structure. A combination square is the most versatile type of square because, in addition to checking both 45- and 90-degree angles, it can serve as a ruler and as a small level.

CHALK LINE A chalk line is ideal for marking long cutting lines on sheet materials and laying out reference lines on a wall, ceiling, or floor. To mark a line, stretch the chalk-covered cord taut between two points. Then lift and snap it down sharply.

TAPE MEASURE A 16- or 25-foot tape measure is sufficient for most jobs, but for laying out distances beyond 25 feet, choose a reel tape. Its end hook should be loosely riveted to adjust for precise "inside" and "outside" readings.

LEVEL To test a horizontal surface for level, place a level on the surface; if the air bubble in the liquid enclosed in the center glass tubing lines up exactly between the two marks, the surface is level. When the level is held vertically, the tubes near each end indicate plumb.

PLUMB BOB To use a plumb bob, hang it by a string and maneuver it until it almost touches the floor. Once the weight stops swinging, it indicates perfect plumb. Mark the point on the floor (it helps to have a partner at the other end).

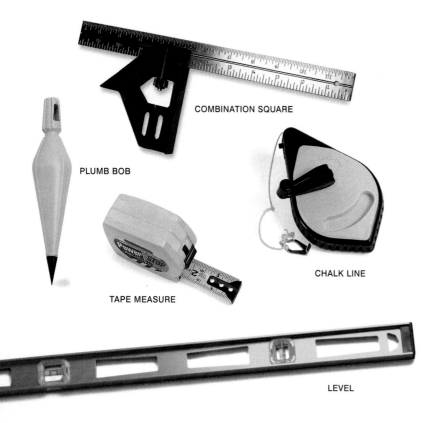

COMBINATION SQUARE

PLUMB BOB

TAPE MEASURE

CHALK LINE

LEVEL

cutting & drilling tools

UTILITY KNIFE A standard utility knife is helpful for many household repair and improvement jobs, including cutting drywall, vinyl flooring, and tile backerboard. Replace the blade frequently to ensure clean cuts.

CROSSCUT SAW A relatively short, multi-purpose crosscut handsaw is convenient for small wood-cutting jobs. Look for a "taper ground" saw; the blade's thickness tapers toward the back and the tip, allowing the teeth to be closer together, which prevents the saw from binding in the kerf (saw cut).

PORTABLE CIRCULAR SAW Used for framing and many other construction jobs, this power saw allows you to make straight crosscuts much faster than with a handsaw and is unparalleled for ripping along the lengths of boards. The most common 7¼-inch model will go through surfaced 2-by framing lumber at any angle between 45 and 90 degrees.

POWER DRILL/DRIVER An electric drill is classified by the biggest bit shank it can accommodate in its chuck (jaws); the most common are ¼-inch, ⅜-inch, and ½-inch. For most jobs, a cordless ⅜-inch variable-speed drill with an adjustable clutch is your best bet; it not only can handle a wide range of bits and accessories, but it also makes an excellent power screwdriver.

RECIPROCATING SAW Ideal for roughing-in or demolition work, the reciprocating saw can be fitted with any of several blades to cut wood studs and joists, lath and plaster, steel pipe, and even nails. For precise control, choose a model with variable speeds.

SABER SAW The saber saw's high-speed motor drives one of many types of blades in an up-and-down (reciprocating) motion; the blade on an orbital model goes forward and up, then back on the down stroke, for faster cuts. A saber saw excels at curves, circles, and cutouts in a variety of materials but can also do straight cutting and beveling. Consider a variable-speed model for more control.

CROSSCUT SAW

UTILITY KNIFE

PORTABLE CIRCULAR SAW

POWER DRILL/DRIVER

RECIPROCATING SAW

SABER SAW

tools & materials

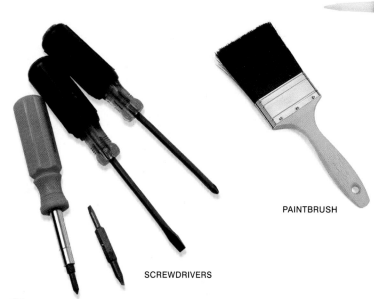

CAULKING GUN

PAINTBRUSH

SCREWDRIVERS

ADJUSTABLE WRENCH

CLAW HAMMER

fastening tools

SCREWDRIVERS The screwdriver vies with the hammer as the most frequently employed tool in a do-it-yourselfer's collection. Since an ill-fitting tip may lead to a burred screw head or gouged work surface, it's important to have small, medium, and large tips in each main shape: standard, Phillips, and square drive. If you'll be driving many screws, save your wrist by using a power drill with a screwdriver bit.

ADJUSTABLE WRENCH You may be surprised at how often you'll reach for a wrench on a repair or remodeling job—to drive lag screws, tighten nuts and bolts, or remove structures such as cabinets and built-ins. A 10- or 12-inch adjustable wrench is an excellent choice for performing a range of jobs.

CLAW HAMMER Hammer faces are either flat or slightly convex. The convex, or bell-faced, type allows you to drive a nail flush without marring the wood's surface. Mesh-type faces are used for rough framing work—the mesh pattern helps guide the nails and keeps the face from glancing off large nail heads. Don't use this face for finish work because the pattern will imprint the surface.

finishing tools

CAULKING GUN For applying caulk and other adhesives, use a caulking gun. For most jobs, a standard-sized one, which uses 10-ounce tubes, is the most convenient and easily handled.

PAINTBRUSH A 3- or 4-inch nylon-bristle brush works well for many types of applications. For painting trim, choose a 2-inch angled sash brush. Spread a brush's bristles to check for good quality—flagging (split ends) and springiness.

materials

At Lowe's you'll discover a vast selection of lumber, fasteners, and other materials for your home improvement projects. To make sorting through the many choices easier, following is a basic primer on the key materials.

LUMBER Lumber is divided into softwoods and hardwoods, terms that refer to the origin of the wood, not its hardness. As a rule, softwoods are much less expensive, easier to tool, and more readily available than hardwoods, so they are chosen for most construction. Hardwoods—which mostly are harder than softwoods—are used where beauty is important, such as for flooring, cabinets, and some trim.

At the mill, lumber is sorted and identified by name and, in many cases, the species and the grading agency. Lumber grades are determined by a number of factors: natural growth characteristics, including blemishes such as knots; defects caused by milling errors; and techniques used for drying and preserving wood that affect strength, durability, or appearance. The fewer the knots and other defects, the pricier a board. To save money on a

STANDARD DIMENSIONS OF SOFTWOODS

Nominal (surfaced)	Actual
1 x 2	¾" x 1½"
1 x 3	¾" x 2½"
1 x 4	¾" x 3½"
1 x 6	¾" x 5½"
1 x 8	¾" x 7¼"
1 x 10	¾" x 9¼"
1 x 12	¾" x 11¼"
2 x 2	1½" x 1½"
2 x 3	1½" x 2½"
2 x 4	1½" x 3½"
2 x 6	1½" x 5½"
2 x 8	1½" x 7¼"
2 x 10	1½" x 9¼"
2 x 12	1½" x 11¼"
4 x 4	3½" x 3½"
4 x 6	3½" x 5½"
4 x 8	3½" x 7¼"
4 x 10	3½" x 9¼"
6 x 8	5½" x 7¼"

project, determine the lowest grade suitable for each component.

Lumber is normally stocked in lengths from 6 to 16 feet and in a broad range of widths and thicknesses. Note that the actual size of surfaced boards and dimensioned lumber is less than what their designations imply due to shrinkage during drying and surface planing (that is, a 2 by 4 is actually 1½ inches by 3½ inches). If you're unsure of actual sizes, either measure or check with a salesperson.

NAILS Common nails, used for rough construction, have an extra-thick shank and a broad head. Drywall nails, a variation, have a thinner shank and a larger, slightly cupped head; annular ring drywall nails, best used for installing drywall on ceilings, have a ribbed shank that grips better. Where you don't want a nail's head to show, choose a finishing nail (after you drive it nearly flush, sink the slightly rounded head below the surface with a nail set). Use hot-dipped galvanized nails where they may be exposed to moisture.

SCREWS Though they're more expensive than nails, screws offer several advantages for certain types of construction. They don't pop out as readily as nails can, and their coating is less likely to be damaged during installation. With screws, you don't have to worry about hammer dents. Screws also are easier than nails to remove when repairs are required.

Usually black in color, drywall screws (also called multipurpose screws) come in many sizes and can be driven with an electric drill or screw gun with an adjustable clutch and Phillips-screwdriver tip. Galvanized deck screws are longer and have a coarser thread; they're suitable for areas that will be exposed to moisture. Because drywall and deck screws are not rated for strength, opt for nails, lag screws, or bolts for heavy construction.

Toggle bolts and hollow-wall fasteners that receive screws allow you to fasten securely to drywall and plaster. Toggle bolts, spreading anchors, and metal threaded anchors are the strongest.

The lag screw (also called a lag bolt) is a heavy-duty fastener with a square or hexagonal head; it is driven with a wrench or a ratchet and socket. Before driving a lag screw, predrill a lead hole about two-thirds the screw's length, using a drill bit that's ⅛ inch smaller than the lag screw's shank. Slide a washer onto each lag screw before driving it.

BOLTS For heavy-duty fastening, choose bolts, most of which are made from steel that is zinc plated. Bolts go into predrilled holes and are secured by nuts. The machine bolt has a square or hexagonal head, a nut, and two washers; it must be tightened with a wrench at each end. The carriage bolt has a self-anchoring head that digs into the wood as the nut is tightened. Bolts are classified by diameter (⅛ to 1 inch) and length (⅜ inch and up). To give the nut a firm bite, select a bolt that is ½ to 1 inch longer than the combined thickness of the pieces to be joined.

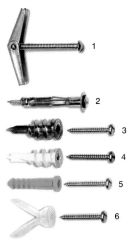

1. Toggle bolt
2. Spreading anchor
3. Threaded anchor (metal)
4. Threaded anchor (plastic)
5. Plastic sleeve
6. Winged sleeve

NAILS, SCREWS & BOLTS

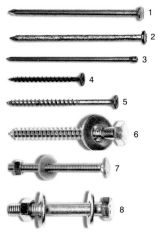

1. Common nail
2. Galvanized nail
3. Finishing nail
4. Drywall screw
5. Deck screw
6. Lag screw and washer
7. Carriage bolt, washer, and nut
8. Machine bolt, washers, and nut

wall & ceiling

improvements

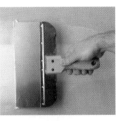

SOMETIMES ALL THAT STANDS BETWEEN YOU AND THE BATH-room of your dreams is a wall. You may want to remove a wall to expand the size of an existing bathroom, reconfigure a wall to relocate a doorway, or add a new wall or partition to create privacy zones within a bathroom.

Understandably, for some people, the prospect of opening up or building walls is daunting. The good news is that the removal or construction of a wall is readily achievable by a moderately experienced do-it-yourselfer. First, however, you must understand some basic structural principles.

Nearly all homes contain two types of walls. Bearing walls are positioned and built to support the weight of the house and the roof. Only an architect or structural engineer is qualified to order the removal of bearing walls, since the weight borne by these walls must be shifted to and supported by other walls or columns before they can be safely removed. On the other hand, nonbearing walls—those that do not bear the structure's weight—can be removed, and built, fairly easily and without these concerns.

The projects on the following pages begin with step-by-step instructions on opening up an existing wall, including removing drywall and plaster and non-bearing wall studs. There are instructions on building a simple nonbearing wall, and on hanging, finishing, and patching drywall. Finally, there are step-by-step instructions on installing interior trim, for that elegant finishing touch.

opening a wall

OPENING UP, MODIFYING, OR ENTIRELY removing one or more walls is relatively easy but guaranteed to make a mess. In addition, you must patch the floor, walls, and ceiling.

Before you remove any wall studs, you must determine whether or not the wall is a bearing wall—part of your home's structural system (see opposite). For more about wall structure, including how to build a nonbearing wall, see page 167.

Be aware that plumbing, wiring, or other mechanical equipment within a wall can make removal far more involved. Rerouting plumbing, in particular, can add significantly to the work. You may not discover the existence of pipes or wires until you've removed the surface material of the wall.

To prepare for demolition, mask off the area with plastic sheeting to prevent the dust from permeating your home, and protect the floor with drop cloths. Turn off the electrical circuits that supply power to receptacles, light switches, and wires in the wall. Pry off any moldings.

To remove gypsum wallboard (drywall), punch through the center of the panel with a hammer and use a prybar to extract pieces. To dispose of plaster and lath, smash the plaster with a sledge hammer, then pry off the lath.

OPENING A WALL

1 Pry any remnants of surface material off the studs of the wall you intend to take out. On the walls that adjoin it, remove the surface material back to the first stud. Pull any remaining nails from all exposed studs.

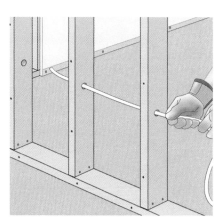

2 Make sure water and electrical circuits are turned off, then remove any wiring or plumbing from the wall; properly cap pipes and terminate circuits. If you're unfamiliar with this type of work, call an electrical or plumbing contractor. (See more about plumbing on pages 174–185 and wiring on pages 186–195.)

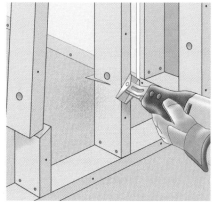

3 Knock out any fire blocks between the studs. Cut through all studs except the end ones a few inches up from the floor. Pull and twist the upper lengths of the studs to free them from the top plate. Using a hammer, knock over the short stud blocks at the base and pry them up. Pull out or cut off any remaining nails.

A doorway opening cut into this wall leads to a generous tiled shower.

WHAT IS A BEARING WALL?

Walls are classified as either bearing or non-bearing. Bearing walls help carry the weight of the house, providing support to floors above and the roof. They should not be removed without a properly engineered method of support—typically a system of beams—to replace them during and after removal. Nonbearing walls help shape a house's interior by defining rooms and serving as conduits for plumbing and electrical systems. They may be removed without compromising the house's stability, though mechanical systems within the walls such as wiring and plumbing must be capped off or rerouted.

All exterior walls are bearing and many interior walls may also be bearing, especially in multilevel homes. Normally, at least one main interior wall, situated over a girder or interior foundation wall, is also bearing. If you are unsure whether or not an interior wall is a bearing wall or how to provide the necessary support during and after removal, consult a local building professional before doing any demolition work.

4 Make a diagonal cut through each end stud at a downward angle, then pry out the two pieces, beginning with the lower half. Pull them free from the top and bottom plates and the anchoring studs in the adjoining walls.

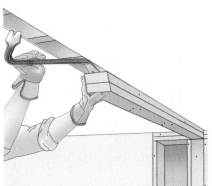

5 If the top plate goes through the adjoining wall, cut it flush with that wall's top plate. Remove the top plate by making a diagonal cut across it, then wedging a prybar between the two halves and pulling downward. Pull out any nails.

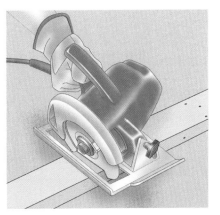

6 As with the top plate, if the bottom plate goes through the adjoining wall, cut it flush at the end first. Then make an angled cut across it, taking care not to cut the floor. Pry up the plate and pull out any nails.

building a wall

SOME BATHROOM PROJECTS INVOLVE building or relocating one or more interior walls. Building a nonbearing interior wall is relatively easy, requiring just basic carpentry skills and tools.

Depending on the nature of your existing floor, walls, and ceiling, you may have to peel away some surface materials to provide for secure attachment at the top, bottom, and ends of the new wall. If the new wall won't butt into studs at the connecting wall or fall directly beneath a ceiling joist, you must install nailing blocks between the framing pieces.

A typical interior wall has a skeleton of vertical 2-by-4 studs that stand between horizontal 2-by-4 base and top plates.

(However, if a wall will contain extensive plumbing, it should be built from 2-by-6 studs and plates.) The framework is typically covered with gypsum wallboard (water-resistant "green" wallboard near a bathtub or shower), tile backerboard and tile, or lath and plaster.

To begin, mark the centerline of the new wall across the ceiling. At each end of the line, measure and mark half the width of the new wall's top plate in one direction. Snap a chalk line between these marks. Plan one stud at each end and, from the end that meets a wall, measure 15¼ inches to locate the inside edge of the first intermediate stud, then 16 inches to the same edge of each additional stud.

ANATOMY OF AN INTERIOR WALL

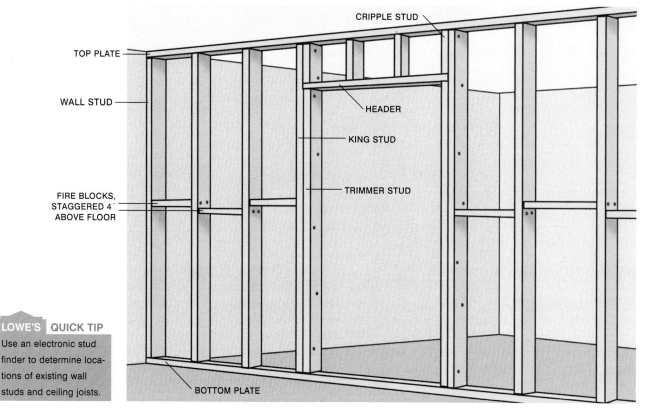

- CRIPPLE STUD
- TOP PLATE
- WALL STUD
- HEADER
- KING STUD
- TRIMMER STUD
- FIRE BLOCKS, STAGGERED 4′ ABOVE FLOOR
- BOTTOM PLATE

LOWE'S QUICK TIP
Use an electronic stud finder to determine locations of existing wall studs and ceiling joists.

BUILDING A NONBEARING WALL

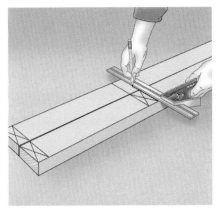

1 On the floor, lay the top and bottom plates side by side. Carefully measure where each wall stud will go and mark with perpendicular lines across the plates, using a combination square so the studs will align perfectly.

2 Locate the joists in the ceiling (here we've shown the drywall on the ceiling removed for clarity). Hold the top plate in position along the guideline marked on the ceiling and nail through the ceiling material and into each joist with two 3½-inch nails (if the new wall runs parallel to the joists, fasten the plate to nailing blocks installed between the joists).

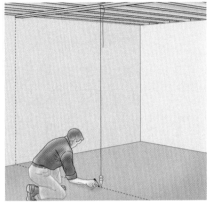

3 Hang a plumb bob from each end of the top plate on the ceiling to just above the floor, then mark the floor to establish the bottom plate's location directly below it. Snap a chalk line along the floor between the marks as a guide for the bottom plate's edge. Nail the plate with 3-inch nails staggered and spaced every 16 inches.

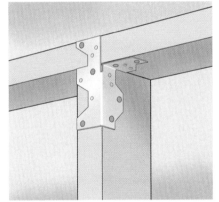

4 Use stud-framing clips, as shown, to install each wall stud. Lift the stud into position and line it up on its mark, flush with the edges of the top and bottom plates. Check plumb using a carpenter's level and nail into place. (Alternately, you can toenail each stud to both the top and bottom plate with 2½-inch nails.)

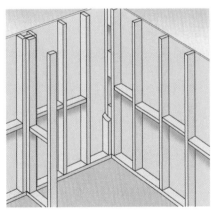

5 Where one wall intersects another, double-up studs, as shown on the left, to receive the intersecting wall. If the wall will turn a corner, frame with two full-length studs that have blocks sandwiched in between, as shown in the cutaway detail at the center of the drawing.

HOW TO FRAME A DOORWAY

- Measure the rough opening for the door and mark its center point. In each direction from the center point, measure half the door's width and mark for the inside edge of each trimmer stud. Measure 3½ inches farther out to mark the inside edges of the king studs.

- Cut the king studs to fit and nail to the plates on each side of the doorway.

- Cut the trimmer studs to the height of the door's rough opening, then nail them to the king studs with 3-inch nails spaced about every 12 inches in a staggered pattern.

- Cut the header and nail it to the trimmers and king studs. Then cut the cripples and nail them to the header and to the top plate.

- Use a handsaw to cut through the bottom plate. Remove the piece within the doorway. Install the door frame.

hanging drywall

BY FAR THE MOST COMMON FINISH material for walls and ceilings is drywall, also called gypsum board; a common trade name is Sheetrock®. Drywall comes in standard 4-by-8-foot sheets and in three thicknesses: ⅜, ½, and ⅝ inch. The most common thickness for finishing a wall or ceiling is ½ inch.

Drywall that is water-resistant is identifiable as such because it comes with a thick blue or green backing. It is a must for bathrooms, especially showers, because of the walls' high exposure to moisture. Both the surface and core of water-resistant drywall are specially treated to protect against humidity. It is almost always used to back ceramic tile.

After purchasing drywall, make sure to store it flat until you're ready to install it. Leaning it up against a wall or other vertical surface could cause it to warp or the edges to crumble.

CUTTING AND INSTALLING DRYWALL

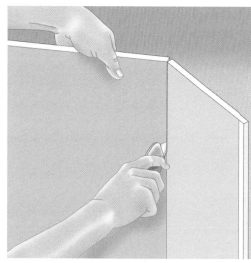

1 Using a pencil and straightedge or chalk line, mark your cutting line across the front paper layer. Score through the front paper with a utility knife, then turn the drywall over and break the gypsum core by bending toward the back. Finish by cutting the back paper along the crease, as shown.

2 When cutting drywall to fit around doorways, windows, outlets, and other surface interruptions, measure out from the adjacent panel and up from the floor to the obstruction, then transfer these measurements onto a new panel and cut. Make small cutouts for outlet and switch boxes about 3⁄16 inch larger than the boxes, and adjust the holes with a perforated rasp if necessary.

cutting drywall

Cutting and installing drywall is fairly straightforward and can be accomplished with only a handful of common hand tools. However, because full panels are heavy and awkward to work with, hanging drywall is far easier with a helper.

If you're covering both ceiling and walls, install the ceiling first—wall panels will fit under the edges of the ceiling panels, helping support them. As shown here, you can use a utility knife to make straight cuts, and a compass saw, drywall saw, or power saber saw to make curved cuts or small cutouts.

If the wall will be painted or wallpapered, you'll need to finish the joints and corners (see page 170), but you may not need to hide joints on installations that serve as a backing for ceramic tile.

fastening drywall

On ceilings, use annular ring nails or drywall screws to fasten drywall panels to joists. On walls, use drywall nails or screws to attach panels to studs, top plate, and bottom plate. Panel joints should be centered against ceiling joists or wall studs and staggered so they don't align with adjacent joints. Before installing wall panels, mark wall-stud locations on the floor and ceiling so you can find them easily after the panels are in place.

Driving screws with a screw gun or drill driver is easiest, particularly for ceilings. Most codes call for spacing fasteners every 8 inches along panel ends, edges, and intermediate supports. Position fasteners at least $\frac{3}{8}$ inch from panel edges.

If you nail the panels, use a bell-faced or drywall hammer to dimple the drywall surface with the final blow on each nail head (but take care not to puncture the paper on the surface). This creates a small divot that will be filled with drywall compound during finishing.

3 To attach drywall to a ceiling, position a pair of stepladders or set up sturdy sawhorses and planks to serve as a low scaffold. Then you and a helper can hold each end of a panel in place against the ceiling joists. Start fastening near the center of each panel, then place a few fasteners at the edges until the panel can support its own weight. Continue until each panel is fully fastened.

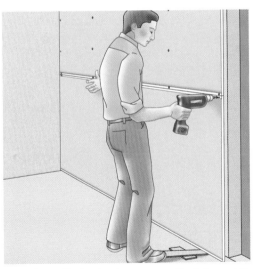

4 For walls, begin at one corner. Push the panel tight against the ceiling, and fasten to the studs. Install the rest of the upper panels, then the lower ones. Force the lower panels tight against the upper ones before fastening.

finishing drywall

The key challenge to finishing drywall is creating invisible seams where panels butt against each other. Although the techniques are simple to master, they require patience and attention to detail.

Cover the joints between panels with paper or self-adhesive mesh joint tape and thin coats of joint compound (commonly referred to as mud). Self-adhesive mesh tape is applied directly over the joint; paper tape must be embedded in a thin coat of joint compound but costs less. Typically, you apply three layers of compound over the tape, each with a progressively wider-blade putty knife. Allow the compound to dry after each coat, then lightly sand.

When you're satisfied with the smoothness and flatness of the joints, let them dry completely, then seal the drywall with primer. Finally, apply the paint or wall covering of your choice.

On inside corners, apply a thin layer of compound to the drywall on each side of the corner and press precreased drywall tape into the corner with a corner tool or putty knife. Then treat as you would any other joint.

Cover outside corners with protective metal corner bead made for drywall. Cut to length and nail through the perforations every 12 inches. Feather out drywall compound (see step 2 below) along the metal edge in three coats the same as you would a regular joint.

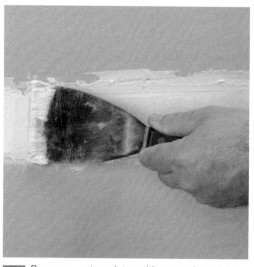

1 Press paper tape into a thin coat of wet joint compound with a wide-blade putty knife, then apply a skim coat over the tape. Also, using a 2-inch putty knife, cover any nail or screw heads with joint compound.

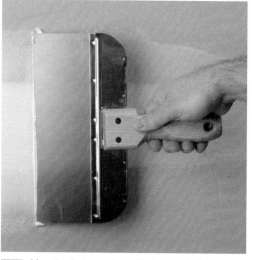

2 After the first coat has dried, sand lightly and apply another coat; allow to dry, sand, then apply the last coat. Use a wider-blade knife with each succeeding coat. Work the compound gently away from the joint to feather it for a smooth transition.

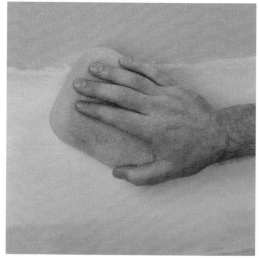

3 Allow the joint compound to dry completely (typically overnight), then smooth the joints with medium, then fine, sandpaper or sanding screen. For a final smoothing, use a damp sponge, which doesn't generate dust.

patching drywall

The method you use to patch drywall will depend on the size of the hole. Small holes are easy to fix, as shown at right, but holes larger than an inch need a drywall patch. One of the simplest ways to patch larger holes is with a drywall repair kit that uses special clips to secure the patch to the wall, as shown in the steps below.

REPAIRING A SMALL HOLE
Tape over small holes with strips of self-adhesive mesh joint tape, then cover with one or more layers of joint compound, allow to dry, and sand.

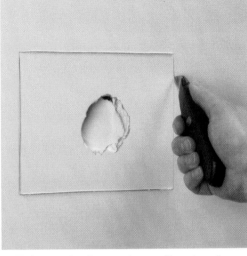

1 Cut out the damaged area with a drywall saw or by making a series of progressively deeper cuts with a utility knife.

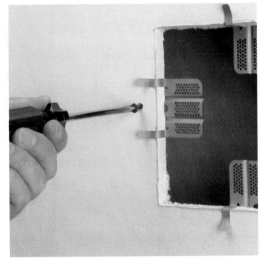

2 Slip the drywall repair clips onto the edges of the hole and screw them into place. Be sure to drive the screw heads slightly below the surface of the drywall.

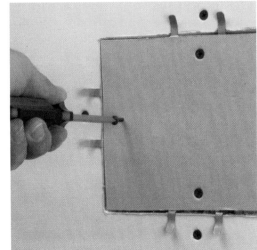

3 Cut a patch from a piece of drywall to fit the hole and attach to the drywall clips by driving screws through the patch into the clips. Finish the seams and cover the clips using the same method as for drywall joints (see opposite).

installing trim

DECORATIVE TRIM SUCH AS CROWN molding is relatively simple to install with a few basic tools—and the results can lift a bathroom with charm, style, and distinctive detailing. Because trim is often installed where two different surfaces or materials meet, it offers an excellent means of hiding joints or separations while producing attractive transitions.

The size and scale of the trim you choose should be in keeping with the size of the room. In situations that allow ornate profiles, several different styles of trim can be combined.

No matter what type of trim you install, you'll use the same methods for cutting, joining, attaching, and finishing it. Whenever possible, prefinish trim before installation, then touch up afterward—an infinitely easier option than masking and painting trim in place.

cutting & joining trim

The simplest way to join two pieces of trim at a corner is with a miter joint, where the ends are cut at a 45-degree angle, then butted together to make a 90-degree corner. You can cut a miter joint with an inexpensive miter box and handsaw, but the preferable tool is a power miter saw, shown opposite.

One difficulty with miter joints at corners is that, in order for the trim pieces to meet precisely, the room's walls must meet

COPING A JOINT

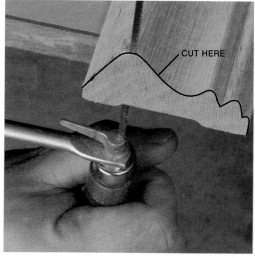

CUT HERE

LOWE'S QUICK TIP
Because few surfaces are perfectly flat, gaps will undoubtedly show up between trim and the wall or ceiling after installation. Seal the gaps with caulk.

1 To cope a joint, place the molding upside down and backward on the miter saw and cut the end at a 45-degree angle. This will reveal the profile you need to cope.

2 Hold the coping saw at a 90-degree angle to the back surface of the molding and cut along the curving contour revealed by the miter-saw cut made in step 1.

1 Locate the wall studs and the ceiling joists, press the flats of the molding against wall and ceiling, drill pilot holes, then drive in finishing nails. Use a hammer and nail set to recess the nail heads.

2 When the ceiling joists run parallel to the wall, you'll have to use one of two alternate methods to secure the top of the molding. The first is to affix the top flat with a bead of construction adhesive.

3 For a more secure hold, cut scraps of wood blocking to fit behind the molding and attach these to the wall studs with 3-inch drywall screws. Attach the molding to the blocking with finishing nails.

at a perfect right angle, and few do. You can try to measure the angle and adjust your cuts accordingly, but this can be both time-consuming and frustrating to get right. A good alternative is to make a coped joint.

Taking its name from the tool used to make it—the coping saw—a coped joint creates a flawless joint at a corner regardless of the angle of intersection. Of the two pieces that make up a coped corner joint, one is left square and butted into the corner, the other is "coped"—cut at a contour to match the profile of the molding, as shown in step 2 opposite. If you're new to coping, practice on some scrap first. Also, cut the molding several inches longer than the finished length needed, to allow for a couple of tries.

In a perfect world, the coped piece will mate seamlessly with its companion piece. Chances are, though, that the coped end will need some fine-tuning. A rat-tail or round file, or a dowel wrapped with sandpaper, works well for making minor adjustments. Check the fit frequently to make sure you don't remove too much wood.

nailing trim

Trim is attached to walls and ceiling with finishing nails. Professional trim carpenters use air nailers, which drive and set a

nail with a pull of the trigger. In addition, an air nailer fitted with a no-mar tip will never ding or dent the molding the way a hammer can. If you're planning to install a lot of trim, consider renting or buying an air nailer. If you're installing a modest amount of trim, however, a hammer and a nail set will work just fine.

After the trim is in place, fill the nail holes with wood putty and touch up with paint if needed.

installing crown molding

Traditionally reserved for public rooms, crown molding is becoming increasingly popular in bathrooms, not only between walls and ceiling but also as a decorative accent at the tops of cabinets or over a shower curtain. As a general rule, choose crown molding that is 3 to 4 inches wide if you have a standard 8-foot ceiling, wider if your ceiling is vaulted.

Cutting and coping crown molding is difficult because the molding comes to a peak on the back side, making it tricky to hold in place. The best way to make accurate cuts is to build a simple cradle for the miter saw. This is nothing more than a couple of plywood scraps screwed together with a cleat attached to the base to hold the molding at the proper angle for cutting.

CUTTING A MITER
A power miter saw is the tool of choice for cutting a miter because it can produce quick, accurate cuts. Just butt the trim piece firmly up against the fence of the saw, align your cut mark with the saw blade, then make the cut. Always wear safety glasses when cutting.

plumbing

improvements

PLUMBING FIXTURES ARE THE MAJOR COMPONENT OF BATH-
rooms large and small, and plumbing is often the most costly
work needed in a bathroom remodel. So critical is plumbing—
and so dire the consequences of a badly done plumbing job—
that many cities require that certain jobs only be done by
licensed plumbing contractors working with permits. Indeed, it
is probably wise to let professionals handle the plumbing if an
entire new bathroom is being built, or for complex jobs such as
installing steam showers and large whirlpool tubs. Tub installation, in particular, can be tricky, since the floors of older homes
may need extra support to bear the weight of today's large,
water-heavy tubs. However, there are a number of plumbing
projects that an experienced, and even not so experienced, do-it-
yourselfer can handle with some ease. In fact, it's worth the time
for all homeowners to learn how to install a simple faucet, since
a plumber may be difficult to employ for such a small job.

   Installation and hookups are the primary plumbing categories.
The commonplace projects presented here include installing (and
hooking up) countertop, wall-mounted, pedestal, above-counter,
and undermount sinks, a faucet, and a toilet.

   The general rule of thumb for working with plumbing is to
make sure the water is shut off at its source before you begin
work. If you are working around electrical wires, particularly
where there might be an old wall heater or exhaust fan, make
sure you have turned off the circuit for that area before you start
to avoid the dangerous mix of water and electricity.

INSTALLING A SINK 176

MOUNTING A FAUCET 182

SETTING A TOILET 184

installing a sink

ONE GREAT WAY TO UPDATE A BATH-room, particularly if you're also replacing a vanity cabinet or countertop, is to install a new sink (actually, the proper term for a bathroom washbowl is "lavatory" or, for short, "lav"). In recent years, plumbing-fixture designers have created a wonderful smorgasbord of high-style bathroom lavatories that turn what was once a mundane fixture into a work of art.

Lavatories are categorized by their support method: countertop-mounted,

A countertop-mounted—or self-rimming—sink drops into a hole cut in the countertop; because its rim hides slight irreg-ularities, installation of this type is forgiving.

pedestal, wall-mounted, undermounted, and above-counter. A popular new varia-tion is the console, which is supported by table-like legs.

For practical bathrooms, lavatory bowls usually combine with a countertop cap-ping a vanity cabinet—a setup that hides the plumbing and provides storage and counter space.

Nearly all lavatory bowls have a pop-up stopper and an overflow hole that pre-vents water from spilling over the sides.

countertop sinks

The instructions opposite are for installing a self-rimming, drop-in bowl—the easiest type to put in. If you're installing a self-rimming sink in a new countertop, you'll start by making a cutout for the bowl. Nearly all sinks are sold with a template for marking this hole. Position the cutout accord-ing to the manufacturer's direc-tions. A single sink is typically centered from side to side and front to back.

When installing a heavy sink (such as a cast-iron unit), you can simply use a bead of plumber's putty rather than adhesive to seal the edges; the sink's weight will hold it in place. If you are installing a recessed or frame-mounted sink, attach the sink with the mounting clips or metal strip included with the unit.

INSTALLING A COUNTERTOP SINK

1 Use the sink manufacturer's template to draw the cutout line on the countertop. If no template is provided, set the bowl upside down on the countertop and trace the outline, then draw a second line about ¾ inch inside that line to serve as your cut line.

2 Carefully drill a ⅜-inch starter hole inside the cut line. Using a saber saw, begin cutting along the line. Before finishing the cut, screw a scrap board longer than the span of the cutout to the center of the cutout to prevent it from falling when you finish cutting. Remove the support after you finish the cut.

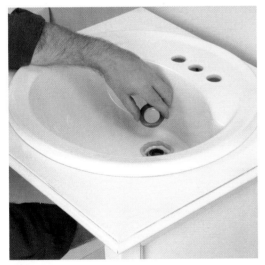

3 Place a bead of plumber's putty around the bottom edge of the drain-assembly housing's lip, then press the housing into the drain hole. Attach the gasket and washer, then tighten the locknut (hold the handles of a pair of pliers in the housing with a screwdriver to prevent the housing from turning while you tighten the locknut). Remove any excess plumber's putty. Attach the tailpiece to the housing with the slip nut and washer.

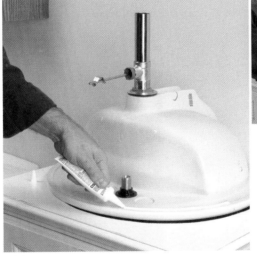

4 If you haven't already done so, install the faucet as discussed on page 182. When the faucet is in place, turn the sink upside down and run a bead of silicone adhesive along the underside of the molded lip (adhesive is included with some sinks). Turn the sink over and carefully align it with the countertop's front edge. Press firmly around the lip to form a tight seal. After the adhesive has set, apply a bead of latex caulk around the edge, then smooth it with a wet finger. Install the pop-up assembly (see page 183, steps 4, 5, and 6).

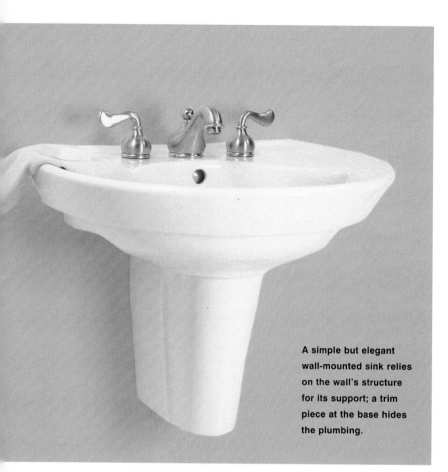

A simple but elegant wall-mounted sink relies on the wall's structure for its support; a trim piece at the base hides the plumbing.

wall-mounted sinks

Wall-mounted sinks are either hung on a metal bracket that is attached to the wall's framing or bolted directly to the framing (as shown here). These sinks come with manufacturer's installation instructions, which should be followed closely.

To provide the proper support for a wall-mounted sink, it's usually necessary to remove a small section of drywall so you can access the wall studs and attach blocking between them. For more about removing wall materials, installing framing, and repairing drywall, see pages 164–171.

Determine where support will be needed, based on the sink's measurements and mounting height (typically 30 inches above the floor). Remove drywall in that area and install 2-by-6 or 2-by-8 blocking between wall studs. Toenail the blocking to the studs with 3½-inch galvanized common nails. Then repair the drywall.

INSTALLING A WALL-MOUNTED SINK

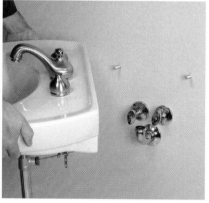

1 Position the mounting plate or sink on the wall and mark the wall through the holes in the plate or sink. Drill pilot holes for lag screws or other fasteners supplied by the manufacturer; if the wall is tile, use a masonry bit. Then install the faucet and drain and pop-up assemblies on the sink (see step 3 on page 177 and steps 4, 5, and 6 on page 183).

2 Use lag screws or other fasteners recommended by the manufacturer to secure the sink or the sink's metal mounting plate to the blocking. After driving in the first fastener, check to make sure the sink or mounting plate is level, then drive in the other fasteners.

3 Connect the P-trap and drain arm to the drain stub-out, then connect the two water-supply tubes to the shutoff valves. Some wall-mounted sinks (like the one shown here) come with a trim piece that hides the plumbing lines. These typically attach directly to the wall framing with lag screws.

pedestal sinks

Pedestal sinks are made up of two parts: the sink and the pedestal (or base). With most, the weight of the bowl isn't carried entirely by the base; a bracket ties the bowl to the wall for additional support. Just as with a wall-mounted sink, you'll want to install blocking between wall studs to help provide that extra support.

Both wall-mounted and pedestal sinks come with the manufacturer's installation instructions, which should be followed exactly, and with the materials necessary for making water-supply and drain connections. The faucet and valves are usually sold separately.

A stately pedestal sink is supported primarily by its base but also bolts to the wall for extra stability.

INSTALLING A PEDESTAL SINK

1 Place the lavatory and pedestal in the desired position. Level and square the assembly, then mark the mounting-hole locations on the wall and on the floor.

2 Drill pilot holes for the fasteners in the wall and floor. If you're drilling tile, use a masonry bit, affixing a piece of tape on the areas to be drilled to keep the bit centered. Next, install the drain assembly and faucet (see pages 181–183).

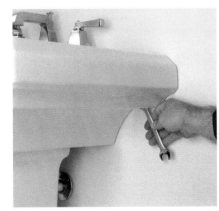

3 Secure the lavatory to the wall with lag screws or other supplied fasteners. Then connect the trap to the drain assembly. With some pedestal sinks, you must rest the bowl on the pedestal, positioned close to the wall, and then hook up the waste and supply lines before securing the bowl to the wall.

4 Once you've secured the bowl, drill a pair of pilot holes in the floor for the bolts that will secure the pedestal to the floor. The pedestal base typically has a pair of notches in the base for these fasteners. Be careful not to overtighten the bolts as this can crack porcelain. If the sink has a nut or rod that connects it to the pedestal, secure the device. Connect the supply lines and install the pedestal.

installing a sink

Though it looks like a shallow bowl sitting on a countertop, this low-profile above-counter sink is set into a hole cut in the counter.

above-counter sinks

An above-counter lavatory is an excellent choice when you want to make a design statement. These stylish lavatories rise above the countertop to create a decorative focal point. They install much like a countertop sink; the only difference is that the hole in the countertop is much smaller. Some above-counter sink manufacturers also provide precut countertops that make installation a snap.

Most manufacturers include complete instructions as well as a pattern for cutting the countertop; be sure to follow the directions precisely.

For information about connecting the sink drain and the water supply lines, see opposite. For directions on installing a pop-up assembly, refer to page 183, steps 4, 5, and 6.

INSTALLING AN ABOVE-COUNTER SINK

1 Locate and cut the opening following the instructions for a countertop sink on page 177. Mount the faucet and drain assembly and temporarily position the sink in the cutout. Check for alignment and clearance and make marks on both the countertop and the sink as guides for installation.

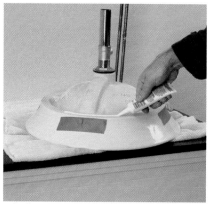

2 Turn the sink upside down and apply a bead of sealant around the underside of the rim, following the directions on the label.

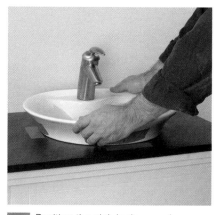

3 Position the sink in the opening, align it with the guide marks, and press down. Allow the sealant to set according to label directions, then connect the drain pipes and water-supply lines (see opposite).

undermount sinks

Recessed, or undermount, sinks are popular because they allow for easy clean-up of the adjacent surfaces and can be installed in practically any type of counter. The method of attachment varies by manufacturer; installation instructions are included with all models. In addition to the bowl, many sink manufacturers also offer countertops that are precut, predrilled, and prefit to work together. All that is required is applying a bead of sealant and tightening some screws.

An undermount sink offers an uninterrupted look and makes the countertop eminently easy to clean.

INSTALLING AN UNDERMOUNT SINK

1 Apply a small bead of silicone caulk (or the sealant provided) around the edge of the bowl, following the directions on the label.

2 Place the countertop upside down, position the bowl and secure it with the screws provided; remove any excess sealant with a clean cloth. Turn the counter over, attach it to the cabinet, and hook up the drain and supply lines.

CONNECTING A SINK

No matter what type of sink you purchase, the drain and water-supply connections are generally installed in this way: Hand-tighten a female adapter onto the drain stub-out at the wall. Slide slip nuts onto the drain arm and the sink's tailpiece. Fit a P-trap in place and tighten the slip nuts by hand. Connect flexible water-supply tubes onto the faucet's tailpieces (see page 183) and route them to the shut-off valves. Tighten coupling nuts with an adjustable wrench. Remove the faucet aerator, turn on the water, check for leaks at the shutoff valves, then turn on the faucet to check for leaks in the drain assembly. Replace the aerator.

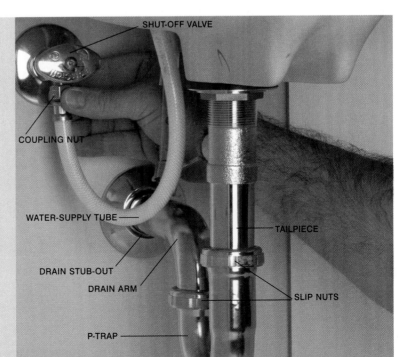

SHUT-OFF VALVE

COUPLING NUT

WATER-SUPPLY TUBE

TAILPIECE

DRAIN STUB-OUT

DRAIN ARM

SLIP NUTS

P-TRAP

mounting a faucet

SOME FAUCETS ARE EASY TO INSTALL; others can be quite difficult. It mostly depends on your access to the plumbing. If you are installing a faucet into a new bathroom sink, chances are it will be simple because you can put in the parts before placing the sink. If the sink is already in place, your only access is from underneath. A tool called a basin wrench can extend your reach, but it's still an awkward task.

This split-set faucet delivers water through a gracefully arching spout flanked by matching valves. With this type of set, valves are typically spaced 8 inches apart.

Whether you buy a single-piece faucet or a split set like the one shown here, be sure your sink or countertop has the appropriate number and sizes of holes for the unit.

To remove an old faucet, first turn off the shut-off valves at the supply tubes. Use a basin wrench to remove the nuts that connect the supply tubes to the faucet tailpieces. Drain the water in the supply tubes into a bucket or bowl. Remove the locknuts and the washers on both tailpieces, then lift out the faucet.

Many new faucets require some assembly before mounting to the sink. If the one you have chosen does, assemble according to the manufacturer's directions. If the sink has a pop-up assembly, remove it before installing the faucet.

When it's time to hook up your new faucet, flexible supply tubes make connecting it much easier because no cutting or fitting of lines is required.

MOUNTING A FAUCET

1 Clean the surface where the new faucet will sit and insert the rubber gasket between the faucet's base plate and the sink top to create a watertight seal. If no gasket is provided, seal the perimeter of the faucet base with plumber's putty, then insert the tailpieces through the holes in the sink top.

2 If your faucet has water-supply tubes already attached to the tailpieces, as shown, feed them through the middle sink hole and press the faucet into position on the sink. From the underside, thread a washer and mounting nut onto each tailpiece (some faucets have a combination washer/nut made of plastic), then tighten the nuts firmly with a wrench.

3 For split-set faucets, like the one shown, you'll need to connect the valves to the spout. Before you connect them with the flexible hoses supplied, wrap a couple of turns of pipe-wrap tape around the threaded ends of the valves and connecting piece. Then thread them on by hand, and finish by tightening with an adjustable wrench.

4 Virtually all bathroom faucets come with a pop-up mechanism that allows you to open and close the drain by pulling up on a lift rod behind the spout. Remove the stopper from the tailpiece, then install the tailpiece as shown so the pop-up port faces the spout.

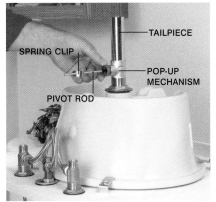

5 Attach the pop-up mechanism to the tailpiece, taking care to thread the pivot rod into the opening at the bottom of the drain stopper. A spring clip on the end of the pivot rod will grip the lift rod.

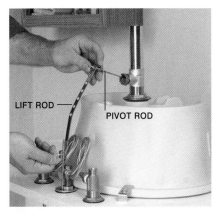

6 Insert the lift rod in the hole in the spout and attach it to the pivot rod via the extension rod supplied. Adjust it so the drain stopper will open and close properly when the lift rod is operated. Connect the faucet's hot and cold supply tubes, bending them gently to meet the shutoff valves. Tighten the compression nuts or flared fittings and turn on the water to clear the lines of any debris and to check for leaks.

setting a toilet

LOWE'S QUICK TIP

Before setting the toilet
in place on the floor
flange, push drinking
straws onto the bolts.
It will be easier to line
up the bolts with the
holes at the toilet's base.

IF ONE OF YOUR TOILETS HAS SEEN better days—or you simply want to update it with a model that is more stylish and efficient—you'll be glad to know that replacing a toilet is an afternoon project. However, if you plan to install a toilet in a new location, you will have to extend supply pipes and drainpipes to the desired spot, a job you may want to leave to a plumbing contractor.

When shopping for a toilet, you'll find many choices (see pages 89–91). The two-piece type that is illustrated here is the most common.

Though most toilets are sold with the necessary gaskets, washers, and hardware for fitting the tank to the bowl, you might need to buy a few parts. These may include hold-down bolts, a wax gasket for sealing the drain, and a flexible water-supply tube for connecting the tank to the shutoff valve.

SETTING A TOILET

1 To remove the old tank, unbolt it from the bowl, using a screwdriver to hold the mounting bolt from inside the tank while unfastening its nut with a wrench from below. Remove the bowl by prying the caps off the hold-down bolts and removing the nuts with an adjustable wrench. Gently rock the bowl from side to side to break the seal between the bowl and the floor, then lift the bowl up, tilting it forward slightly to avoid spilling any remaining water.

2 Stuff a rag into the drainpipe to prevent sewer gas from escaping into your home. Using an old putty knife, scrape the wax gasket remains from the floor flange. (If the old hold-down bolts and/or the floor flange are damaged, replace them, too.)

3 Turn the new bowl upside-down on a cushioned surface. Place a new wax gasket over the horn on the bottom of the bowl, facing the tapered side away from the bowl, as shown. If the wax gasket has a plastic collar, install it so the collar is away from the bowl, first checking that the collar will fit into the floor flange. Apply a thin bead of caulk around the toilet base.

Before beginning installation, turn off the water at the shutoff valve or at the house's shutoff valve. Flush the toilet to empty the bowl and tank, and sponge out any remaining water. Disconnect the water-supply tube from the shutoff valve, drain the water from the tube into a bucket, then unscrew the coupling nut on the supply tube at the bottom of the tank.

If the hold-down bolts that fasten the toilet to the floor are corroded to the extent that you can't remove the nuts, soak the bolts with penetrating oil or cut them off with a hacksaw. When you bolt the new bowl to the floor, be very careful not to overtighten the nuts as this can crack the porcelain.

Behind the sleek styling of this two-piece toilet is a hard-working flushing mechanism that utilizes a siphon action to assist gravity. Pre-installed bolts ease joining the tank and bowl.

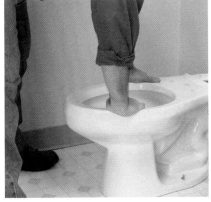

4 Remove the rag from the drainpipe. Gently lower the bowl into place atop the flange, using the bolts as guides. Press down firmly while gently twisting and rocking. Using a level, check that the bowl is straight; use plastic shims if necessary to make minor adjustments.

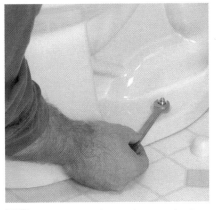

5 Hand-tighten the washers and nuts onto the bolts. Then alternately tighten them with a wrench until the toilet is seated firmly on the floor. Snug up the hold-down nuts, but don't overtighten—this can crack the bowl. Fill the caps with plumber's putty and place them over the bolt ends.

6 If necessary, assemble the flush valve inside the tank and tighten the large spud nut at the center. Place the rubber tank cushion on the bowl. Position the tank over the bowl and tighten the nuts and washers onto the mounting bolts. Hook up the supply tubes and open the shutoff valve.

electrical

improvements

A BATHROOM'S ELECTRICAL DEMANDS ARE NOT ESPECIALLY unusual or complicated unless you are installing complex bath appurtenances such as whirlpool tubs or saunas. For the most part, improvements involve installing lights, switches, receptacles, and the like.

Though it's best to leave more involved wiring jobs to professionals, certain tasks can be accomplished with relative ease and safety by a do-it-yourselfer with some wiring experience and understanding of electrical systems. The projects presented on the following pages—wiring receptacles, wiring switches, installing a vanity light, and installing a combination light/fan fixture—are all of this type.

While the projects themselves are not taxing, you should keep some things in mind as you begin to work with the existing electrical systems. First, all bathroom electrical receptacles should be protected by ground fault circuit interrupters (GFCIs). For more about these, see page 189. Also, the outlets in many older homes may not be grounded; today, proper grounding is required by code and is an absolute safety must. Be especially cautious if you find electrical wires near plumbing, since a leak may present a serious hazard. If you are in any way unsure of what you are confronting, stop and call in an electrician. Other cautionary notes will appear in the margins of this section—be sure to look them over before beginning your project. And, of course, study all of the step-by-step instructions carefully.

Basic electrical work requires a few relatively inexpensive tools. If you need to purchase the tools, or want to upgrade what you have, look for specialized insulated hand tools that are colored bright orange and marked "1000" for their ability to withstand current up to 1,000 volts.

WIRING RECEPTACLES 188

WIRING SWITCHES 190

INSTALLING A VANITY LIGHT 192

INSTALLING A BATH FAN 194

wiring receptacles

OLDER BATHROOMS OFTEN HAVE ONLY one or two electrical outlets, a real problem for modern families whose power needs extend to nightlights, hair dryers, electric shavers, and more. Not surprisingly, adding new receptacles is usually a priority when remodeling a bathroom.

Receptacles are rated for voltage and amperage—typically 120 volts and either 15 or 20 amps. When you're replacing a receptacle, look at the back of the existing one to find the voltage and amperage ratings so you can install an identical part.

Receptacles are also marked either AL-CU or AL with a slash through it. The former may be used with aluminum or copper wire, the latter with copper only.

Take note that most municipalities require all bathroom receptacles be protected by GFCIs (ground fault circuit interrupters). You can protect the entire circuit by installing a GFCI circuit breaker at the main electrical panel, or you can install individual GFCI outlets. For more about GFCIs, see sidebar opposite.

Don't replace an old-style two-prong outlet with a new, grounded three-prong receptacle without first having an electrician run a ground wire to the electrical box. Without it, the circuit will be unsafe.

WIRING A RECEPTACLE

1 Be sure the power to the circuit is turned off. Remove the outer sheath of insulation and all separation materials from the cables inside the box. Strip insulation from the wire ends and use a wire nut to join the grounding wires with a grounding jumper. For a metal box, screw a grounding jumper to the box.

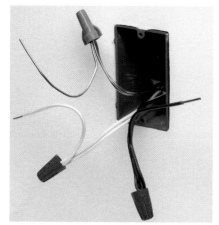

2 For a middle-of-run receptacle, twist together hot (black) wires with a short black jumper wire and cap with a wire nut. Do the same with the neutral (white) wires. If you are wiring an end-of-run receptacle, it will have only single white, black, and bare incoming wires, which connect directly to the receptacle.

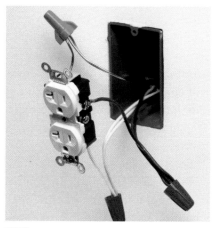

3 Attach the hot jumper to one brass screw terminal, and the neutral jumper to the silver terminal. Secure the grounding jumper to the green grounding screw. Tighten unused screw terminals. (For an end-of-run receptacle, connect the incoming wires to the terminals.)

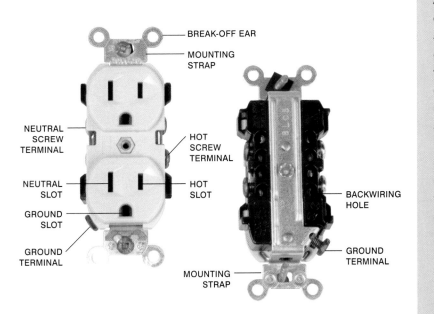

BREAK-OFF EAR

MOUNTING STRAP

NEUTRAL SCREW TERMINAL

HOT SCREW TERMINAL

NEUTRAL SLOT

HOT SLOT

BACKWIRING HOLE

GROUND SLOT

GROUND TERMINAL

GROUND TERMINAL

MOUNTING STRAP

DUPLEX RECEPTACLE

This is the most common type of receptacle, with two places for plug-ging things in. On the back of some receptacles are three terminals: brass, silver, and green. The brass terminals are for hot wires, the silver for neutral wires, and the green for ground. To make a connection, wrap the stripped wire clockwise around the terminal and tighten the screw against the receptacle body. Most new receptacles have push-in termi-nals at the back, directly behind the screw terminals—you just push the straight end of the stripped wire into the hole.

BUILT-IN SAFETY: GFCI

A ground fault circuit interrupter is an electronic device that monitors a circuit for ground faults and shuts it down when one is detected. A ground fault is what happens when the current flowing into a circuit and the current flowing out of the circuit are not the same; that is, some cur-rent is flowing outside the circuit, creating a haz-ard to property or to persons.

You can protect an entire circuit with a GFCI cir-cuit breaker at the main panel, or protect individual outlets with GFCI receptacles. A GFCI receptacle will protect the devices plugged into it as well as additional receptacles "forward" on the circuit.

Wiring a GFCI is similar to wiring a standard receptacle except the terminals are labeled "line" and "load." To protect a single location, attach the incoming pair of black and white wires to the "hot" and "white" (neutral) terminals on the line end. To protect several outlets, the incoming wires are connected the same way, but the outgo-ing pair of black and white wires attaches to the load end. Be aware that such multiple-outlet pro-tection is susceptible to erroneous tripping when normal electrical fluctuations occur—which can be a nuisance since you will have to reset the cir-cuit every time.

4 Carefully fold the wires into the box and screw the receptacle to the box. Be careful not to crimp a wire, which can create a short, or open, circuit. Before tightening, be sure the receptacle is straight. If it isn't flush, shim it out, using the break-off flat metal rounded ears located at both ends of the receptacle.

5 Screw the faceplate to the recepta-cle, as shown, using the screw included with the faceplate. Be careful not to overtighten the screw—this can crack the faceplate. GFCI receptacles usually have two screws (see detail).

LOWE'S SAFETY TIP

Before working on any electrical wiring, turn off the circuit breaker or remove the fuse to dis-connect the circuit. Test the bare ends of the wires with a voltage tester to make sure the wires are not charged.

wiring switches

AS BATHROOMS HAVE GROWN IN SIZE and function, so have their lighting needs. It's common for today's hi-tech bathrooms to employ everything from in-shower spotlights to vanity and makeup lights. Because updating a bathroom's lighting scheme nearly always calls for replacing, updating, and adding light switches and dimmers, these pages offer methods for installing and wiring these devices.

By far the two most common types of switches used are the familiar single-pole variety that controls one or more lights from one location, and the three-way switch, which allows you to turn lights off and on from two locations. To tell whether a switch is a single-pole or a three-way, count the number of terminals (flat screws on the sides). A single-pole switch will have two brass terminals and a green ground terminal, while a three-way will have three brass terminals and a green ground terminal. Most new switches also allow for connections via push-in terminals at the back.

Switches are rated for a specific voltage and amperage. Whenever you replace a switch, look on the back for these ratings and purchase one that matches them.

Unlike receptacles, switches are wired only with hot (charged) wires, which means they open and close the hot leg (normally the black wire) of a circuit to allow current flow to the light.

INSTALLING A SINGLE-POLE SWITCH

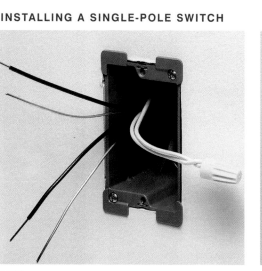

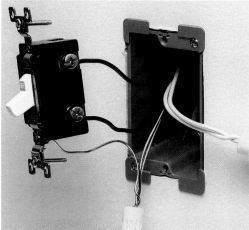

1 Be sure the power to the circuit is off. Remove the outer insulation and separation materials from the end of the nonmetallic cable. Strip the insulation from the wire ends. Twist together the bare ends of the neutral (white) wires, if any, and cap with a wire nut.

2 Twist together the grounding (bare) wires with a short piece that will run to the switch's grounding screw, and join with a wire nut (for a metal box, run a third bare wire from this wire nut to a clip or screw connected to the box). Screw the hot (black) wires to the screw terminals; it makes no difference which hot wire goes to which terminal.

WIRING A DIMMER

Dimmer switches can be wired into existing circuits in the same manner as the switches they replace. Dimmers come for both single-pole and three-way switches and for incandescent, fluorescent, and halogen lights. When selecting one, make sure it's designed for the type of lighting you want to control. Wiring a dimmer is easy because most come with short jumper wires that connect to the existing wiring via wire nuts—connections are the same as for switches.

THREE-WAY-SWITCH WIRING

A three-way switch has two brass terminals and one darker terminal labeled "common." To wire a pair of three-way switches, first be sure the power is off, then connect the hot wire from the service panel or subpanel to the darker terminal on one switch. Connect the hot wire from the lighting fixture to the darker terminal on the other switch. Wire the remaining terminals by running hot wires from the brass terminals on one switch to the brass terminals on the other switch.

3 Fold the wires behind the switch. Carefully push the wires into the box and guide the switch's screws into their holes. Start tightening the screws; check that the box is aligned vertically, then finish tightening the screws. If the switch doesn't sit flush with the wall, break off one or more of the rounded ears at the corners to use as shims.

4 Finally, attach the faceplate to the switch using the screws included with it. Several types of faceplates are available in metal and plastic to suit your decor and various configurations of switches. With a plastic faceplate, don't overtighten the screws as this can crack the plastic. Last, turn the power on to the circuit.

LOWE'S QUICK TIP

Both "hot" supply wires that enter a box to connect a switch are usually black. Occasionally, a white or red wire is used instead. In such cases, wrap a piece of black electrical tape around the white wire (or paint it black) to indicate that it's hot.

installing a vanity light

Wall-mounted sconce lights, installed at each side of a mirror or medicine cabinet, provide flattering, even lighting.

ONE SIMPLE WAY TO BRIGHTEN UP A bathroom is to install new lighting. Replacing a vanity light also allows you to upgrade a key element of your bathroom's decor. Vanity lights come in a wide variety of shapes and sizes; all are easy to install over an existing electrical box, requiring less than an hour from start to finish. Some electrical boxes are located directly above a mirror or medicine cabinet, others—like the one shown here—are at each side.

Before purchasing a fixture, make sure it will fit the space, without bumping into an adjacent wall or interfering with a mirror or trim. Follow the manufacturer's instructions precisely.

Before you begin any work, turn off the power to the existing fixture at the electrical service panel. Remove the globe or diffuser and the bulb(s). Unscrew the retaining nut that holds the decorative cover plate onto the electrical box. If the old fixture doesn't come off easily, run the blade of a utility or putty knife around the edges of the plate to free it from caulk or paint. Disconnect the wiring and set the fixture aside.

INSTALLING A VANITY LIGHT

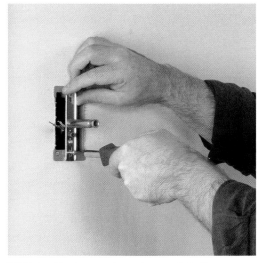

1 In older homes, incandescent light fixtures are often mounted directly to an electrical box. Electrical codes now require that the fixture be mounted to a flat metal bar called a mounting strap that is secured to the box. Most new fixtures include the mounting strap and screws.

2 Before installing the fixture, inspect the wires coming out of the box. If the ends are nicked or tarnished, cut them and strip off ½ inch of the insulation with a wire stripper. Then, following the manufacturer's instructions, attach the fixture's wires to the circuit wires with the nuts provided.

3 All lighting should be properly grounded. This is particularly important in a bathroom, where water is present and the chance of electrical shock is higher than in other rooms. In hooking up the ground wire, make sure to follow the manufacturer's instructions. On many lights, you'll hook the ground wire to the mounting strap, as shown here.

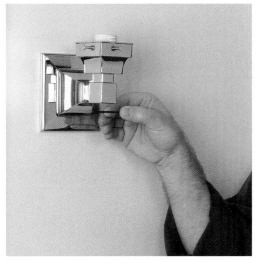

4 Mount the fixture to the box as directed by the manufacturer. Finally, screw in the appropriate bulbs, making sure their wattage does not exceed the maximum allowable for the fixture. Attach the diffuser, which typically is held in place with a decorative cap or retaining nut. Tighten only friction-tight to avoid cracking the diffuser.

LOWE'S QUICK TIP

To create strong but gentle light that doesn't cast shadows, choose a fixture that utilizes halogen bulbs and has a frosted diffuser.

installing a bath fan

BECAUSE HEAT PLUS MOISTURE EQUALS mold and mildew, every bathroom needs a way to combat this combination. The most efficient way is to exhaust bathroom air outside. Most new homes come with a fan already installed; older homes—if they have a fan at all—usually have one that is underpowered. Whether your home is new or old, check the rating of your fan. If it is under 80 CFM (cubic feet per minute), replace it with a stronger one.

Replacing an existing fan with a new one is about as simple as replacing a vani- ty light (see pages 192–193). Just make sure the new unit will fit in the existing opening and that it uses the same type and size of ducting.

Installing a new fan requires cutting a hole in the ceiling where the overhead light fixture is and routing vent pipe to an exterior wall, where you'll cut through and connect a vent cap. In this situation, you will want to purchase a fan that has a built-in light. If the vent work (see the facing page) is beyond your skill level, call in a heating contractor.

SETTING A BATHROOM FAN

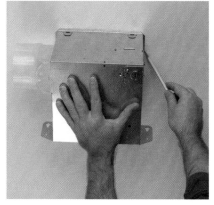

1 Turn off the power to the existing fix- ture at the service panel. Remove the old fixture. Position the template or housing on the ceiling so it aligns with the ceiling joist. Trace around the template or housing to locate the opening. Alterna- tively, if you have access from above, position the housing or template next to the joist and trace around it.

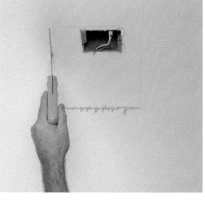

2 Cut out the opening according to the manufacturer's directions using a drywall saw, saber saw, reciprocating saw, or utility knife.

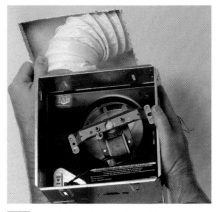

3 Attach the ductwork and insert the housing up into the opening. Secure the housing to the joist with the fasteners provided. Make sure to fill all the mounting holes with fasteners to reduce vibration and ensure noise-free operation.

VENTING OPTIONS

There are two common ways to route ductwork to vent bathroom air outside: through the ceiling and out through an exterior wall, or through the ceiling and out through the roof. (You can also buy a fan that vents directly through an exterior wall, but this typically requires running a new electrical line to the wall.) Of the two ceiling options, a vent through a wall is less likely to leak.

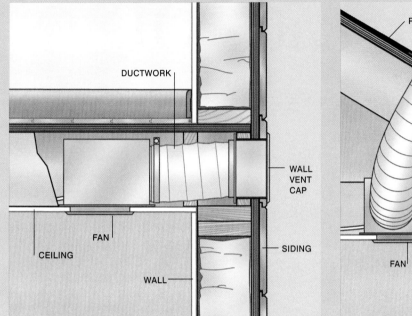

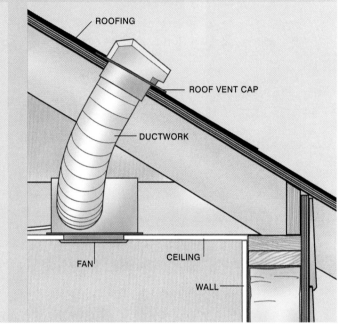

4 Connect the fan unit to the existing wiring following the manufacturer's wiring diagram. Be sure the electrical circuit is turned off when doing all work.

5 Attach the fixture to the housing and attach the grille to the fixture with the fastener provided.

6 Screw in a light bulb and attach the diffuser; this will generally just snap in place. Finally, run the ductwork, making as few turns as possible (see above). Mark the location for the vent cap and cut out the hole. Apply a bead of silicone caulk around the perimeter of the cap and slide it in the opening. Fasten the cap to the wall with galvanized screws. Connect the ductwork to the vent cap and test the system.

surface & cabinet

improvements

A BATHROOM'S TYPICALLY GLEAMING SURFACES—FLOOR, countertops, and cabinets—are strikingly apparent. In fact, the smaller a bathroom is, the more prominent its surfaces. As a result, all that's needed to completely transform some bathrooms is a fresh coat of paint on the cabinets, or a new countertop or floor. Replacing the vanity, medicine cabinet, and fixtures are also simple ways to give an old bathroom a bright new look and improved functionality.

Luckily, all of these projects are among the easiest for do-it-yourselfers, especially when the tasks are pursued with patience and a measure of exactitude. And because these kinds of remodeling tasks can be expensive to have performed by a professional, doing the work yourself can amount to significant savings.

On the following pages, you will find step-by-step instructions for laying resilient, ceramic tile, and wood floors; hanging and updating cabinets; tiling a countertop and installing a surface-mount medicine cabinet and accessories. Tool requirements are few, although laying floors and setting tile do demand some specialized equipment. When it comes to laying floors, a true first-timer might want to opt for inexpensive, easy-to-install resilient tile. It also helps to be something of a perfectionist—measuring and remeasuring is critical, since one mistake can throw off the whole project. Because surface work is, by its nature, very visible, and most bathrooms tend to be tight quarters, flaws will be readily apparent.

These jobs also are nicely suited for two compatible workers. Working with another helps allay any tediousness—particularly when it comes to laying ceramic tile—and has the benefit of giving you a second set of eyes.

laying resilient flooring

ONE OF THE MOST POPULAR BATHROOM flooring materials is resilient tile, a surface that is highly water-repellent, moderately priced, slip-resistant, and easy to install. Tiles are uniform in size—the standard is 12 inches square—and fit together snugly without grout lines. They can be cut with a utility knife and a straightedge. Some tiles have self-adhesive backs, but these tiles tend to be thinner, more limited in selection, and may not form as sure a bond as the types set with an adhesive compound. Complete instructions for installing self-adhesive tiles are included with their purchase. The following directions are for installing the type applied with an adhesive.

For a quality job, the substrate must be clean, flat, and very smooth. A plywood subfloor or an older vinyl floor that meets these requirements will serve.

Before you begin, remove everything atop the floor and pry off the shoe molding along the base of walls; remove baseboards only if there isn't any base shoe molding. If you'll be covering old resilient flooring, glue down any loose corners or edges. Smooth embossed flooring or any

1 With a notched trowel held at a 45-degree angle, spread adhesive over the substrate using long, sweeping strokes that overlap by about 1 inch. Trowel away any excess immediately.

2 After waiting the proper amount of time, usually about half an hour, carefully position the first tile at the intersection of the working lines. Be sure to get this one right because all the others will align to it.

3 Continue installing tiles, aligning the edge of each with a working line or adjacent tile. Let the tiles fall into place (sliding them may force adhesive up between them). Check alignment and make adjustments if necessary every couple of tiles. From time to time seat the tiles with a rolling pin or by walking on them.

dips or bumps by troweling on an emboss-
ing leveler, then sanding it.

If your floor is very irregular, cover
with plywood flooring underlayment,
made for this purpose. The edges of these
panels interlock; if you must cut panels,
run these along the walls. Stagger corners
so that four pieces don't come together in
one place. Note that plywood underlayment is marked with small crosses; drive a
screw or pneumatically shoot a flooring
staple at every cross mark. Set the heads
of all fasteners below the surface.

You can walk on the tiles immediately
after installing them, but you must not
step on the adhesive, so do a dry run first.
You can begin either at the center of the
room or at one wall. Starting at the center
is generally best, and necessary if the
room is out of square or if you've chosen
tile with a pattern or design. Lay out
working lines that intersect at a right
angle in the middle of the room (see the
illustration at top right). Start at a wall
only if two adjacent walls meet at an exact
90-degree angle.

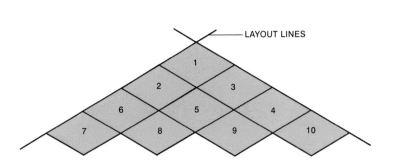

LAYOUT LINES

When you're satisfied with your layout,
read both the tile and adhesive manufacturers' directions, paying particular attention to the time it takes the adhesive to
dry. Apply adhesive evenly and sparingly
with a notched trowel (see the adhesive
directions for the proper notch size). Allow it to become translucent and tacky,
but not dry, before installing the tiles. Use
soapy water or mineral spirits (depending
on the type of adhesive) to clean up any
excess as you work.

Establish perpendicular working lines across the center of the floor. Begin at the intersection of the two working lines and install tiles in the order shown, working toward the edges so that tiles around the border will be equal in size.

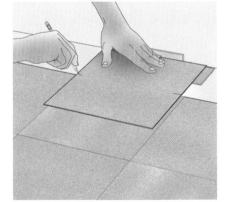

4 To figure out how much to cut off a
border tile, turn it upside down in the
correct direction over its future location
and press it against a ¼-inch spacer at
the wall, making sure it does not touch the
adhesive. With a pencil, mark both edges
for the cut. Score a single line with a
straightedge between the two marks, then
hold both sides of the tile firmly and bend
it until it snaps.

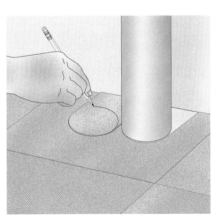

5 To fit tile around pipes or obstacles,
cut a pattern from cardboard, then
use a contour gauge or compass to transfer the pattern onto a tile. To cut irregular
shapes, use a sharp utility knife, scissors,
or tin snips if the tile is pliable or can be
made so by warming with a hair dryer. If
necessary, cut out a separate piece and
glue it in place. Caulk around pipes and
cover with a flange.

LOWE'S SAFETY TIP

Resilient flooring
installed before 1986
may contain asbestos,
which can be a serious
health hazard if the
fibers are released into
the air. Experts recom-
mend removal by a
specialist or covering
the old floor with ply-
wood underlayment
before installing the
new flooring.

laying a tile floor

CERAMIC TILE IS ONE OF THE MORE difficult flooring materials to install, but, when the job is done, the results are well worth the effort. The method shown on these pages is for laying tile in a thinset mortar base (tile can also be installed with adhesive), the approach recommended by most professional tile setters.

Before putting in a new floor, you will have to remove the toilet and any pedestal sinks. (To do this, simply reverse the installation directions on pages 184–185 and 179, respectively.)

Next, gently pry up the quarter-round shoe molding along the base of the walls. (Baseboards do not need to be removed unless there is no shoe molding.) As you remove the molding, number the pieces with a pencil so you can easily replace them later. Finally, remove all doors.

preparing the base

So that it won't crack over time, ceramic tile must be laid on a firm, solid, flat base. Several types of existing subflooring can provide such a base, including concrete slab and wood or plywood. But a wood or plywood base must be strong enough not to flex when you jump on it. For this reason, a plywood or solid-wood subfloor is typically covered with ½-inch cement backerboard or ½-inch plywood underlayment. The combined thickness should be at least 1¼ inches.

Cover wood-strip and plank flooring with ½-inch plywood underlayment since neither is smooth enough to serve as a backing for ceramic tile. Similarly, cushioned resilient flooring is too springy to serve as a base, so remove it or cover it with plywood underlayment. (Your old

INSTALLING BACKERBOARD

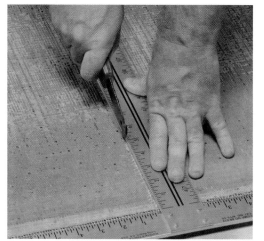

1 Sweep debris from the floor and lay down the sheet to be cut. Measure for the cut, then subtract ¼ inch for the rough edge. Cut the panel with a cement-backerboard knife, guiding the blade along a framing or drywall square, as shown.

2 Turn the sheet upside down and, holding the board flat on one side of the scored line, snap the other side upward. Pick the sheet up on its side, score the back of the cut, and snap the piece back to complete the cut. Smooth the rough edge with a tile stone.

resilient floor may contain asbestos; refer to the safety information in the Lowe's Safety Tip on page 199.)

New ceramic tile can be applied over old tile that is in good condition. To improve adhesion of the thinset, roughen the old tile's surface with an abrasive disk mounted in an electric drill (wear a dust mask), then clean the surface with a commercial degreasing agent.

installing **backing**

Stagger the sheets of cement backerboard or underlayment so they do not fall directly over joints in the subflooring; also stagger the pieces so that four corners do not come together. If using plywood, interlock the edges; if using backerboard, leave a ⅛-inch space between the panels. Allow a ¼-inch gap between plywood or backerboard panels and the wall or baseboard. Drive a screw or pneumatically shoot a flooring staple at every cross mark on plywood underlayment. Fasten cement backerboard with special backerboard screws, setting all of the heads below the surface.

layout **tips**

A tile layout can start either from perpendicular working lines at the center of the room or from one corner. Begin at the center if the room is badly out of square or if you've chosen tile with a pattern or design. You'll have to cut tiles along all four walls, but they will be of equal size. Start at a corner only if the adjacent walls meet at an exact 90-degree angle. Then you'll only have to cut tile for two walls. Plan your tiling so you will never have to step on recently laid tiles—this often means starting at the far end of the room and working toward the door.

To mark layout lines for the tile, snap two perpendicular chalk lines where you want to begin. To ensure that your first line of tiles will be straight, temporarily screw in a batten, or a long, straight board, next to a working line.

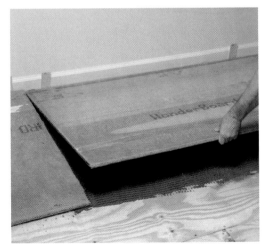

3 Sweep the floor again and mix thinset mortar according to label directions. Spread the mortar on the floor using a ¼-inch square-notched trowel. Lay the sheet in the mortar carefully. Drive screws through the sheet into the joists every 6 inches (or as recommended by the manufacturer).

4 Lay fiberglass mesh tape over the joints and, using the flat edge of a trowel, spread a fine layer of thinset mortar over the tape. Feather out the thinset on either side, and smooth away any high spots. Once the thinset hardens, the surface is ready to tile.

LOWE'S QUICK TIP

To find out whether a room has perfectly square corners, lay a half sheet of plywood on the floor with its factory edges 1 inch away from a corner's adjacent walls. Measure to see if either wall goes out of square along its length.

laying a tile floor

Establish the working lines you'll use as guides for the first tiles you lay, as shown on page 201. Butt the first row of tiles up to a batten fastened along one of the lines. Once the mortar begins to harden, remove the batten.

cutting tile

To mark a cutting line, use a pencil, a crayon marker, or a felt-tipped marker. For 90-degree marks, use a combination square. Angles can be transferred from a wall to a tile with an adjustable T-bevel, and irregular shapes can be transferred with a contour gauge.

Always wear safety glasses or protective goggles when cutting. Cut straight lines using a snap cutter or, if the area you are tiling is large, consider renting a wet saw with a diamond blade. Stone, terra-cotta, cement-body, and some porcelain tiles should be cut only with a wet saw. (Consult the tile dealer to determine which technique to use for specific porcelain tiles.) Cut curves or small cutouts with a nibbling tool. For interior cuts, first drill a hole using a masonry bit, then enlarge the hole with a rod saw.

installation tips

Open all the tile boxes and check for uniform color before you begin installation. If the tile is dusty, wash and dry it since dust will keep the adhesive from forming a strong bond.

Make a dry run before you begin setting tiles in thinset. This will help keep the number of cut tiles to a minimum.

For most tile, use gray thinset mortar with a liquid-latex additive. For glass tile, marble, or other tile that is translucent, use white thinset mortar.

Mix only as much as you can use in about 30 minutes (less if the weather is warm and dry). Follow label directions precisely. The mortar should be wet enough to pour, and just thick enough to stick to a trowel for a second or two when held upside down.

Pay close attention to the mortar's open time (the amount of time it remains workable) so you don't end up racing to set the tile. Once the mortar begins to harden, adjusting tiles is almost impossible.

Use tile spacers to maintain properly sized grout joints. As you go, clean off any excess mortar with a damp rag. About

LAYING A TILE FLOOR

1 Use the smooth edge of a notched trowel to spread mortar on the floor next to a batten. Comb the area with the notched edge, holding the trowel at a consistent angle, as shown. Use sweeping strokes to create an even bed.

2 Align the first tile with the batten or working lines and set it in place. Make sure you do not slide it more than about an inch. Then set several more, inserting spacers at every corner. Avoid pressing down when placing the tiles.

3 Continue placing tiles. Once a section of floor is finished, bed the tiles by setting a short block over two or more tiles and tapping with a rubber mallet. Periodically sight across the tiles to make sure they're forming a level plane. Remove any excess mortar as you go.

FOUR WAYS TO CUT TILE

To cut with a snap cutter, position a tile firmly against the cutter's front guide, lift the handle, and push or pull to score a line. Push down on the handle to snap the tile in two.

Use a snap cutter to make small cutouts. First score the lines using a snap cutter, then take small bites out of the cutout area with the nibbling tool. Smooth edges with a tile stone.

To make a cutout with a rod saw, which turns corners easily, hold the tile firmly in place, with the area to be cut overhanging the work surface. Saw with steady, moderate pressure.

To use a wet saw, slide the tray all the way toward you and position the tile against the guide. Turn on the saw. Holding the tile firmly, slide it gently forward against the blade.

every 10 minutes, pick up a tile you've just set; mortar should cover the entire undersurface. If it doesn't, scrape the mortar off the floor and reset the tile with new mortar.

After installing all the tiles, remove the spacers, finish cleaning up any excess mortar, and allow to set up for at least 12 hours before walking on the floor.

Prepare grout by adding water sparingly to powdered grout, mixing small quantities at a time. Be sure all particles are thoroughly moistened and there are no lumps. Mix in a liquid grout sealer. Always wear rubber gloves when mixing grout, as the lime in it is caustic.

Let the grout cure for the time specified by the manufacturer. Then, if you've used a cement-based grout, apply a grout sealer for extra protection, following the manufacturer's instructions. Wipe any sealer off the tiles before it hardens.

4 To mark a border tile for a straight cut, place a spacer equal in thickness to the grout lines against the wall. Set the border tile on top of the adjacent whole tile and precisely align their four edges. Set another whole tile on top, then slide it against the spacer. Use the edge of the top tile to guide the cutting line.

5 Pour about 1 cup of grout onto the floor at a time. Holding a laminated grout float nearly flat, force the grout into the joints using sweeping back-and-forth strokes in two or more directions. Then, tip the float up and, using it like a squeegee, drag it diagonally across the tiles to clear away the grout.

6 Before the grout dries, wipe the tiles with a large damp sponge (rinse frequently), using light pressure and a circular motion. Then smooth and slightly recess the grout joints with a damp sponge. Let the grout dry until a haze appears on the tiles, then polish the tiles with a soft cloth. Apply a grout sealer.

laying a WOOD floor

BECAUSE WOOD EXPANDS AND CON-
tracts with moisture—and can rot if it's left
in contact with water for a long period of
time—many homeowners shy away from
choosing wood flooring for bathrooms.
Actually, wood can be a warm, beautiful
flooring option for bathrooms as long as
it's given a sturdy, protective finish and is
dutifully maintained.

Traditional strip or plank wood flooring
is fastened down to subflooring and then
sanded and finished. Newer prefinished
wood floorings are fastened down the
same way but do not require finishing.
Unless you're experienced in sanding and
finishing wood floors, you'll do well to
choose the latter type because floor sanding is incredibly dusty work, and a drum
sander, in the hands of an amateur, can
leave visible marks and ridges on the floor.

a **base** for flooring

New wood flooring should be laid on a
clean, smooth, level, structurally sound
base. Depending on the particular flooring, this base may be a previous floor covering, an existing wood floor in good condition, a new plywood subfloor, or even a
moisture-proofed concrete slab.

By installing wood over an existing
floor, you bypass the messy job of removing the old flooring and you gain instant
soundproofing and insulation from the old
floor. A disadvantage to leaving old flooring in place is that you must correct any
irregularities in it. Also, the new floor may
raise the flooring level too much, making

the transition to a hallway or an adjoining
room awkward.

Whether or not you're installing over
old flooring, begin by removing doors and
base shoe molding (remove baseboards
only if there is no shoe molding). Number
the molding pieces so you can easily
replace them when you're finished.

If you plan to remove the old flooring
before laying the new, do so at this stage.
Install subflooring over the exposed joists,
centering the long edges of ¾-inch
exterior-grade plywood with a tongue-
and-groove edge on the joists. With 2-inch
cement-coated or ring-shank nails, nail
every 6 inches along the long edges and
every 12 inches along intermediate joists.
Stagger panels so no four corners come
together in one place. Leave ⅛ inch
between panels and ½ inch next to walls
(where molding will cover the gap) to
allow for expansion.

installation steps

Before installing wood flooring, stack it
indoors for a few days to allow the wood
time to adjust to your home's humidity
level. Plan to install the flooring perpendicular to the floor joists. Mark the
positions of the joists along a wall for
reference, as shown in step 2 on page
206, and cover the subfloor with a layer
of 15-pound asphalt felt to provide some
moisture protection and minimize squeaks.
Mark the centerline of the room (as discussed in step 1).

If the room is seriously out of square,

This warm wood floor sets a striking stage for beautiful fixtures in a seaside bath.

position the tongue of the first row parallel to the centerline and rip the groove side at an angle parallel to the wall.

During installation, you'll find it's helpful to lay out several rows of boards, staggering them so no end joint is closer than 6 inches to an end joint in the next row. As you install the strips, cut pieces (at least 8 inches long) to fit at the end of each row; allow a ½-inch gap at the wall.

Use a radial arm saw or power miter saw to cut the boards. When blind-nailing with a hammer and finishing nails, don't try to drive the nails flush—the indentations will show. Instead, leave each nail-head projecting up about ⅛ inch, then place a nail set sideways over it along the upper edge of the tongue and drive the nail home by tapping the nail set with your hammer. Finally, use the tip of the nail set to recess the nail's head flush with the wood.

"FLOATING" LAMINATE FLOORS

Laminate flooring, a European import now widely popular in the United States, can mimic the look of traditional wood floors as well as tile, stone, and other materials. The surface of laminate flooring is a highly detailed photographic image that is overlaid with transparent, extremely durable plastic laminate (similar to the material used for countertops). The base material is a wood-composite product, often medium-density fiberboard (MDF). A backing layer is then added to prevent moisture seepage, which can damage the planks.

Laminate floors are installed as floating floors, meaning they are not secured to the subfloor. Instead, the individual tongue and groove planks—typically about ⅜ inch thick—are fastened to each other with an adhesive. Some types are installed over a thin foam pad.

Laminate floors can be installed over existing flooring materials, including wood, tile, and vinyl; carpeting must be removed. Each manufacturer of laminate flooring products offers complete installation instructions. When installing a laminate floor in a bathroom, you must be particularly careful to join and seal the edges of the planks according to the manufacturer's directions to prevent moisture from seeping between or below the planks. Before installing laminate flooring in a bathroom, check the product's warranty to be sure it covers this type of installation.

1 Cover the subfloor with a layer of 15-pound asphalt felt, overlapping seams by about 3 inches. Tack down with a staple gun. Measure the room's width at two or more points to establish an accurate centerline, and snap a chalk line parallel to your starting wall. Working from the joist marks along the walls, snap chalk lines to mark the locations of the support members.

2 To indicate the edge of the first row of flooring, snap another chalk line about ½ inch from the starting wall exactly parallel to your centerline. This ½-inch gap between the flooring and the wall will allow for expansion; it will be covered by base shoe or baseboard molding.

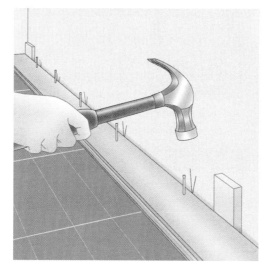

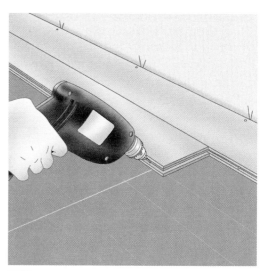

3 Choose the longest boards or widest planks for the first row. Near the wall, where the nailheads will be covered by a base shoe, drill pilot holes for 1½-inch finishing nails, then face-nail the first row through the plywood subflooring to the floor joists or sleepers. Use a nail set to recess the nails below the surface.

4 Blind-nail this and the next two rows by hand. Drill pilot holes at a 45-to-50-degree angle through the tongues, centered on each joist or sleeper, at the ends and every 10 inches along the lengths. Fasten with 1½-inch finishing nails. Use a nail set to finish driving each nail.

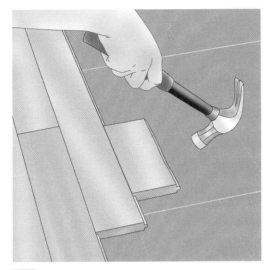

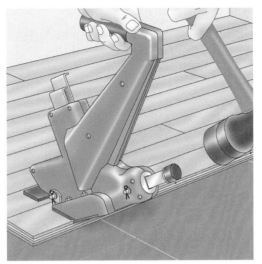

5 When installing the second row and every row thereafter, move a short piece of flooring along the edge and give it a sharp rap with a mallet to tighten the new row against the previous row before nailing. Remember that end joints in two adjacent rows should not be closer than 6 inches; end joints should also not line up over a joint in the subfloor. If you're installing a wide-plank floor, some manufacturers recommend leaving a crack the width of a putty-knife blade between planks for expansion.

6 If you're installing flooring over a large area, use a flooring nailer once you've installed the first three rows. Slip it onto the board's tongue and, using a heavy rubber mallet, strike the plunger to drive 2-inch nails or staples through the tongue into each joist and into the subfloor midway between joists. Be very careful to avoid scratching or otherwise damaging the flooring.

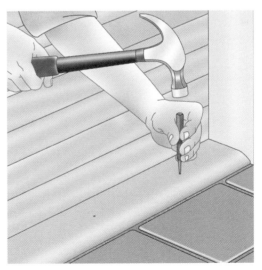

7 When you reach the final row, use a block and a pry bar to wedge the last boards tightly into position. Drill holes and face-nail boards where base shoe or baseboard molding will cover, using the reference marks along the wall to locate the joists. Set the nailheads below the surface using a hammer and nail set.

8 If your new floor will cause a change of level to a hallway or adjoining room, install a reducer strip for a smooth transition. This strip, milled with a rounded or beveled top, fits onto the tongue of an adjacent board or the ends of perpendicular boards. It can also be butted against the edges or ends of grooves. Face-nail the reducer strip at the edge of the floor, set the nailheads below the surface, and fill with wood putty. Last, reinstall the base shoe or baseboard molding.

setting cabinets

FEW ELEMENTS AFFECT THE FEEL AND functioning of a bathroom as much as the cabinetry. Installing cabinetry does not require professional skills, but an eye for precision is all-important. If you're installing more than one base cabinet, you will need to make sure the units are level,

This console cabinet is a breeze to install; methods are the same as those used for a standard base cabinet.

plumb, and flush with each other so that they will work properly and look right. To ensure this, the first cabinet must be level and plumb, both from side to side and front to back, because all of the other cabinets will be aligned to it. A corner cabinet should be installed first. Plan to put in cabinets after rough wiring and plumbing but before new flooring.

If the cabinets don't arrive assembled, put them together according to the manufacturer's directions, with the exception of the doors, shelves, and drawers. For pre-assembled cabinets, remove these parts, labeling them to take the guesswork out of reassembly.

The wall to which you are affixing the cabinets should be smooth, level, and clean. Place a long straightedge against it to make sure it's flat. Mark any bumps or bulges. During installation, tap short pieces of wood shingles, or shims, beneath and/or behind the cabinets as necessary to make slight adjustments. If the irregularities are significant, compensate for them by using a scribe rail (see the Lowe's Quick Tip opposite).

Upper cabinets should be fastened securely to wall studs, particularly if they will be loaded with heavier items such as small appliances or big containers of bathroom cleansers. Most cabinets have a support rail that runs across the back; screw through this or through a strong part of the cabinet. For each cabinet, use at least three screws that penetrate the wall studs by a minimum 1½ inches.

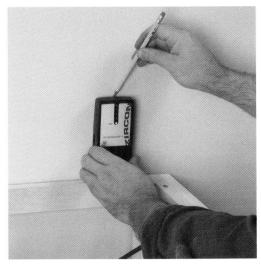

1 Using a stud finder, locate the wall studs to which the cabinet will attach. Mark the stud locations on the wall with a pencil where you'll be able to see the marks after the cabinet is in place. Draw straight vertical lines to indicate the center of the studs.

2 Level the cabinet from front to back and from side to side (if necessary, use shims to raise it to the high point of the floor or to adjust its position). Note: On some vanities, such as the one shown, adjustable levelers built into the legs eliminate the need for shims.

3 Drive screws through the cabinet back rail (and shims) into the wall studs. Trim the shims with a sharp chisel or knife so they won't be visible when the countertop is in place. With the sink and faucet set installed, position the countertop and attach it to the cabinet from underneath.

updating cabinets

If your cabinetry provides adequate storage but seems a little shabby or dated, all it may require is a facelift. Changing the hardware and repainting the cabinets can completely alter the look of your bathroom (see page 211).

Cabinet doors that droop or shut poorly may just need the hinges repaired or changed. First, tighten the screws. If a screw won't tighten, remove it, squirt a little white glue into the hole, and insert broken-up wooden toothpick pieces to fill the hole up (wipe off any excess glue). When the glue is dry, use a utility knife to cut the toothpick pieces flush with the surface, and drive the screw into the refurbished hole (you may first have to drill a small pilot hole).

LOWE'S QUICK TIP
A scribe rail is a length of wood shaped to serve as a buffer between a wall with an irregular surface and a cabinet. Use a simple compass to trace the wall's surface onto the rail, then trim it to ensure a tight fit.

HANGING A WALL CABINET

A wall-mounted cabinet can provide generous storage without taking up floor space; it must be fastened securely to the wall studs.

1 To install wall-mounted cabinets, start by determining their positions and drawing a level horizontal line on the wall where the bottom of each cabinet will be located. Double-check your layout by lightly penciling the cabinets' dimensions and placement on the wall.

2 Align the top edge of a temporary 1-by-3 support rail with the line for the bottom edge of the cabinets and drive three or four 2-inch screws through it into the wall studs.

3 Drill pilot holes through the sturdy part of the cabinet back or its support rail into wall studs. Screw the cabinet to the wall using two screws that are long enough to penetrate the studs by at least 1½ inches.

Decorative hinges can also add a new design element to your cabinets. They come in a vast range of materials and sizes so you're sure to find replacements that will fit your cabinets and perk up and/or revamp their appearance.

If your cabinet doors always seem to hang open, you can switch to self-closing hinges that keep the door closed without requiring a separate catch. European frameless-style cabinets and doors that are out of alignment may simply require hinge adjustment. These hinges, usually mounted directly to the interior cabinet side so they are hidden when the door is shut, are self-closing and can be adjusted with only the turn of a screw.

An equally easy repair is adjusting drawers that don't close well. This problem usually can be solved by reattaching or replacing the drawer's glides.

For the smoothest, most trouble-free drawer opening and closing, purchase prefabricated metal ball-bearing glide sets that attach to the drawer bottom or sides, depending on your drawer's construction. Follow the manufacturer's instructions for proper installation.

PAINTING CABINETS

Whether you want to lighten up dark and dingy cabinets or enliven things with bold colors, paint can provide an instant makeover for most types of cabinets. Because paint doesn't adhere well to laminate and melamine cabinets, it isn't a good idea to paint these types.

Painting with a short (4- or 6-inch) foam roller lets you cover the faceframes with a single stroke and quickly handle the wider doors. Satin enamel paint is an excellent choice because it covers well and is easy to clean.

Remove all screws, hinges, knobs, and pulls and set aside ones you'll be reusing. Empty drawers and pull them out. Thoroughly clean all surfaces with TSP (trisodium phosphate). Rinse completely with fresh water and allow to dry. Fill any holes with wood putty and allow to dry. Then sand all surfaces with 150-grit open-coat sandpaper and vacuum to remove any dust and sanding grit.

Mask off all adjacent surfaces and position drop cloths to protect counters and floors. Paint the parts in this order: faceframes, inside surfaces of the doors, drawer fronts, fronts of the doors. If additional coats are required, allow the first coat to dry overnight and lightly sand all surfaces with 220-grit wet/dry sandpaper. Vacuum thoroughly, then apply the paint.

1 Mask off all adjacent surfaces and position drop cloths to protect countertops and flooring. Begin by painting the faceframes, then turn your attention to the doors and drawers.

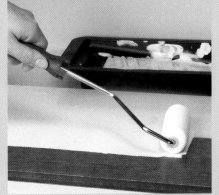

2 Next, paint the insides of the doors and, while you allow them to dry, paint the drawer fronts. Then paint the fronts of the doors.

3 Once the painted surfaces are dry, install the drawers and attach the doors. Carefully lay out and drill holes into a jig and through the doors at the desired hinge location. Finally, install the pulls.

tiling a countertop

CERAMIC TILE MAKES AN EXCELLENT surface for bathroom countertops because it resists moisture and stains, cleans up easily, and serves durably for years. If you've never installed ceramic tile before, you'll discover that tiling a countertop is an ideal first-time project because it's a relatively small, horizontal surface. For more advanced tile work, such as tiling the walls surrounding a shower or bathtub, ask a Lowe's customer service representative about helpful do-it-yourself workshops.

Before selecting your tile, measure your countertop carefully. Calculate the number of tiles of a given size required to cover it, allowing for any specialty tiles, such as those needed for edging or a backsplash. (Manufacturers make a number of edge tiles, the most common being the bullnose shown in step 5 on page 215.) To allow for cutting and breakage, order slightly more than you need; the rule of thumb is to buy 10 percent extra. Once you've made your purchase, lay out the tile on the countertop to ensure you have enough for the job and to see where you will need to make cuts.

building the substrate

The surface that receives countertop tiles needs to be solid, level both front to back and side to side, and able to withstand moisture. Its front edge must be thick enough to accommodate the bullnose tiles or edging you have chosen. In most cases, a layer of ¾-inch plywood topped with ½-inch or ¼-inch cement backerboard will do the job.

During your planning, you may be able to modify your countertop's dimensions slightly in order to minimize or eliminate cutting of tiles.

Before you begin work, cover base cabinets with plastic sheeting or construction paper to protect them from damage and falling mortar. Also, position a drop cloth on the floor.

For information about various types of sinks, see pages 92–96. If you intend to install a flush-mounted sink, do so before

A ribbon of triangular ceramic tiles—cut from squares—provides a decorative accent along the backsplash of this handsome countertop.

BUILDING THE SUBSTRATE

1 Attach the plywood to the top of the cabinets by driving 1⅝-inch galvanized deck screws (which resist rusting) through the plywood into the cabinet base every 6 inches. If you'll be setting a sink bowl into the counter, cut a hole for it following the manufacturer's instructions and check to make sure the sink fits it. (Attach a flush-mounted sink before adding the backerboard.)

2 Cut backerboard pieces to fit and lay them out in a dry run. Seams between pieces should be offset from plywood seams by at least 3 inches. For a flush-mounted sink, bring the backerboard up to the sink edge. Using a ¼-inch notched trowel, spread just enough latex-reinforced or epoxy thinset mortar over the plywood for one backerboard piece at a time. Lay the backerboard in the thinset, and drive 1¼-inch backerboard screws in a grid, spaced approximately 6 inches apart.

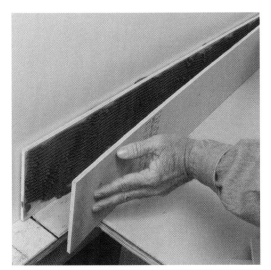

3 Cut pieces of backerboard to accommodate the thickness and width of the backsplash if the backsplash will be tiled with radius bullnose or quarter-round trim at the top. Butter (smear mortar on) the back of the strips with thinset mortar, and press into place against the wall.

4 Apply fiberglass mesh tape to the backerboard joints and wrap the front edges of the backerboard and plywood with the mesh tape. Do not apply mesh tape where the backsplash meets the countertop.

the backerboard is in place. If you're planning an undermount sink, install it after the backerboard or after the tiling is finished. A typical self-rimming sink is installed after the countertop.

Cut the plywood pieces so they overlap the front edge of cabinets by about an inch. Install them with the factory edges facing out. Check the entire surface to make sure it is level as you attach the plywood; if necessary, remove screws, install shims, and re-drive the screws.

Cement backerboard is easy to cut and install: You simply scribe and snap it, then attach it to the plywood foundation with special galvanized screws. For more about installing cement backerboard, see pages 200–201. Once the backerboard is in place, cover the screw heads with thinset mortar, tape the seams with fiberglass mesh tape, and fill in with thinset mortar.

installing the tiles

For complete information about cutting tile, see page 203. If the tile is particularly hard, you may need to cut it with a wet saw, which can be rented. When you cut a tile, a sharp edge will result. This edge is not only easily damaged but difficult to wipe clean. If possible, position all cut edges at the back of the countertop, where they can be covered by backsplash tiles or molding.

Do a dry run before you prepare the mortar. Place the tiles on the substrate where they will go, with plastic spacers for the grout lines, and make adjustments as needed. Aim for a symmetrical look, with no narrow slivers of cut tiles.

If you're using edging tiles, mark a line along the edge of the countertop to allow for the tiles plus a grout joint, then place a guide strip along this line and temporarily attach it to the countertop with nails. Lay out the field tiles from the edge of the strip to the back of the countertop, using a straightedge to align them.

For a countertop that turns a corner, start the layout at the inside corner. If the layout ends with a very narrow sliver, slightly widening the grout lines may solve the problem. In cutting the tiles, take into account the width of the grout lines on either side.

Mix as much latex-reinforced or epoxy thinset mortar as you can use in half an hour. If the mortar starts to harden while you are working, throw it out and mix a new batch.

Follow the label instructions when mixing grout for the installed tile. Once the grout becomes firm, wipe off excess with a damp sponge. Allow residual film on the surface to dry to a haze, then buff with a clean, soft cloth. Apply a sealer after waiting the time specified by the manufacturer (typically two to four weeks).

INSTALLING THE TILES

1 Spread latex-reinforced or epoxy mortar onto no more than 2–3 square feet of the backerboard at a time, using a ¼-inch square-notched trowel. Hold the trowel at a consistent angle for even application and scrape away any globs of thinset.

2 Begin laying tiles by working out from the corner. Press a tile firmly into the mortar, wiggling it slightly as you press down. Continue to fill in tiles on either side of the first tile; use plastic spacers to create even gaps for the grout.

3 Once all the full tiles are in place, cut tiles as necessary to fill in; remove the spacers. Hold a full-size tile in place and, using a permanent marker, draw a line for the cut. Refer to page 203 for information on cutting tile.

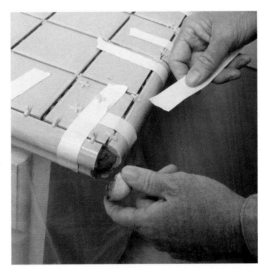

4 For a backsplash, back-butter the tiles (smear mortar onto their back faces), or comb mortar onto the backerboard strip with the trowel. Raise the bottom backsplash tiles the width of a grout line with spacers. If there is a small quarter-round piece at the top (as shown), nest it in mortar packed into the space above the backerboard strip. Hold the pieces with masking tape until they set.

5 Remove the edging strip guide, then back-butter and position the edging pieces so they butt up against the full tiles. Press down and wiggle to set. Maintain consistent grout joints with spacers and hold tiles in place with masking tape. Allow the mortar to set up overnight, then apply the grout with a grout float as discussed on page 203.

installing a medicine cabinet

This surface-mounted cabinet, with hinged, mirrored doors, offers a quick and easy way to provide storage for bathroom paraphernalia.

MOST MEDICINE CABINETS ARE MOUNTED on the wall surface or in a recess. Installing a surface-mount medicine cabinet is about as simple as hanging a picture. Even if your existing cabinet is mounted in a recess, you can upgrade to a larger surface-mounted type.

Medicine cabinets come with sliding, hinged, or pivoting doors, in one, two, or three sections, and a vast number of materials and styles to match almost any decor.

The most important thing to keep in mind when installing a surface-mount medicine cabinet is that it can become quite heavy when full so it must be attached securely to the wall studs.

INSTALLING A MEDICINE CABINET

1 Hold the medicine cabinet in place, centered over the sink and level, and trace around it lightly with a pencil. If necessary, have someone help you with this step.

2 Locate and mark the positions of the studs within the marked area, using a stud finder, and transfer these to the inside of the cabinet.

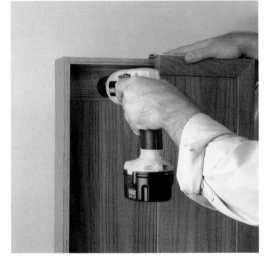

3 Drill four ⅛-inch-diameter holes through the back panel of the cabinet at the marked locations. Most cabinets have a cleat or hanging rail at the top of the back to help support the cabinet's weight; make sure the top two holes are drilled through this cleat.

4 Secure the cabinet to the wall studs with the screws provided. If you can't hit wall studs at each location, use hollow wall fasteners.

hanging accessories

This chrome-plated towel holder's sweeping curve is as decorative as it is functional.

ALTHOUGH THEY'RE FREQUENTLY AN afterthought, the accessories in a bathroom—the towel bars, soap dish, toilet paper holder, and so forth—can tie together the room's design elements, or create discord. Many fixture manufacturers have created accessories to coordinate with their sinks, toilets, and tubs to take the guesswork out of selection.

No matter the type of accessory, it needs to be fastened securely to the wall. In a perfect world, there would be a wall stud wherever you wanted to attach an accessory, but this is rarely the case. The alternative is to use some type of hollow-wall fastener.

These fasteners are designed to "grip" the wall when the fastener is driven in. There are four common types: plastic inserts, self-tapping aluminum inserts, Molly bolts, and toggle bolts. Plastic inserts are driven into a hole drilled in the wall and expand when a screw is inserted; they're best for light-duty applications. Aluminum inserts are driven directly into the wall, then accept a screw to secure an accessory. Molly bolts work well for a specific wall thickness (such as ½-inch drywall). When a machine bolt is driven into the installed bolt, "wings" expand to grip the wall. Toggle bolts require a relatively large hole in the wall but do an excellent job of supporting medium- and heavy-duty loads.

Whenever possible, try to attach at least one mounting screw of an accessory to a wall stud.

HANGING ACCESSORIES

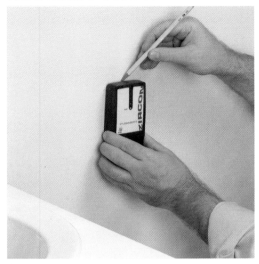

1 Position the accessory roughly where you want it, then use an electronic stud finder to locate studs in that area. Lightly mark their positions with a pencil.

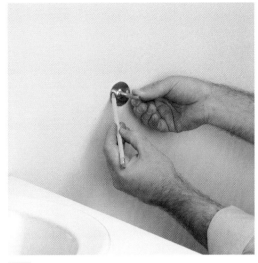

2 Reposition the accessory so at least one mounting screw can be driven into a stud and mark through the accessory's mounting hole onto the wall. Drill appropriate-sized holes for either screws or hollow-wall fasteners.

3 Install hollow-wall fasteners as needed. Make sure that the decorative plate of the accessory will cover the fastener when mounted.

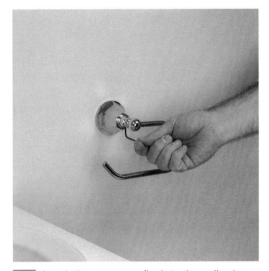

4 Attach the accessory firmly to the wall using screws or bolts. Take care not to overtighten as they can strip out. Note that many accessories (including the one shown here) don't attach directly to the wall; instead, a mounting plate is screwed to the wall, and the accessory is then attached to the mounting plate with a set screw.

credits

DESIGN

19 (TOP): Jeffrey Tohl, Architect.

19 (BOTTOM): Virginia Schutte and Ken Hayes.

21 (TOP LEFT): Macaluso & Associates Architects/Michael Macaluso.

23: Mark Hutker & Associates, Architects.

33: Weston & Hewitson Architects.

34: Quinn Evans Architects.

35 (BOTTOM): Scholz & Barclay, Architects.

38 (LEFT): Pamela Pennington and Tsun-Yen Wahab, Pamela Pennington Studios.

42 (RIGHT): Katherine Murray Associates, ASID.

43 (LEFT): Jeff Luth, Soldano/ Luth Architects.

45 (TOP LEFT AND BOTTOM): Mark Creedon, M2 Studio.

50 (BOTTOM RIGHT): Sandy Oster Interiors.

52: Stephen G. Smith, Architect.

54 (TOP): Ray Kappe, Architect.

56: Interiors by M&S/Marilyn and Stephanie Wolfe.

60 (BOTTOM RIGHT): Country Floors/ Susan Kelly.

61: Mark Hutker & Associates, Architects.

63 (LEFT): Axel Berg, Builder.

65: Weston & Hewitson Architects.

66 (BOTTOM RIGHT): Whipple Callender, Architect.

70 (TOP LEFT): Scholz & Barclay, Architects.

THANKS

Fixtures and cabinetry used in the photographs on pages 176–185, 192–193, and 208–210 courtesy of American Standard.

PHOTOGRAPHY

American Bath Factory, 77 (MIDDLE), 81 (ALL EXCEPT TOP). American Olean, 75 (BOTTOM), 101 (TOP), 103 (TOP LEFT), 118, 120 (LEFT). American Standard, 1, 6, 21 (BOTTOM), 89, 92, 94 (TOP RIGHT), 102 (TOP RIGHT), 104, 141, 162, 205. Amerock, 111 (BOTTOM). Atlas Homewares, 110 (RIGHT), 112 (SECOND FROM TOP; SECOND FROM BOTTOM AND BOTTOM). Bali, 132 (RIGHT). Barta, Patrick, 43 (LEFT). Bates & Bates, 95 (TOP ROW MIDDLE). Belwith International, Ltd., 111 (ALL EXCEPT TOP LEFT AND BOTTOM). Bertch, 106 (RIGHT). Broan–NuTone, 127 (ALL). Cable, Wayne, 158 (BOTTOM), 197 (SECOND FROM TOP AND THIRD FROM BOTTOM), 200–203 (ALL), 213–215 (ALL). Caverly, Todd, photographer, Brian Vanden Brink Photos, 66 (BOTTOM RIGHT). Chen, Ken, 68. Cielo baths by Whirlpool Corp., 7, 78, 82 (ALL), 174, 196. Congoleum Corp., 116, 117. Contractors Wardrobe, 85 (MIDDLE). Crane Plumbing, 79 (ALL BOTTOM EXCEPT BOTTOM RIGHT), 80 (TOP TWO), 83 (ALL EXCEPT BOTTOM), 84 (BOTTOM FOUR), 85 (TOP THREE), 90 (ALL), 91 (BOTTOM TWO), 93 (BOTTOM FOUR), 94 (TOP THREE), 95 (TOP LEFT; TOP SECOND FROM LEFT; TOP SECOND FROM RIGHT AND TOP RIGHT), 100 (BOTTOM LEFT). Delta Faucet Co., 99 (TOP RIGHT AND MIDDLE). DuPont Corian Solid Surfaces, 94 (BOTTOM), 101 (BOTTOM). DuPont Zodiaq Quartz Surfaces, 102 (BOTTOM LEFT). DuPont Stainmaster, 121. Ennis, Phillip, 21(TOP LEFT), 50 (BOTTOM RIGHT), 56, 60 (BOTTOM RIGHT). Ex-Cell Home Fashions, Inc., 155 (BOTTOM THREE). Fitzgerrell, Scott, for Hometips, 159 (SECOND FROM TOP; THIRD FROM BOTTOM AND BOTTOM), 160 (TOP LEFT). Formica Corp., 100 (TOP RIGHT), 103 (BOTTOM), 120 (RIGHT). Glen, Laurey W./ SPC photo collection, 27. Good Earth Lighting, Inc., 126 (MIDDLE). Gray, Art, 44 (RIGHT). Grohe, 77 (BOTTOM), 86 (BOTTOM RIGHT), 87, 88 (MIDDLE), 98 (BOTTOM), 112 (TOP). Gutmaker, Ken, 37, 46, 54 (BOTTOM). Hadley, Jamie, 11, 42 (RIGHT), 45 (TOP LEFT AND BOTTOM), 73. Hartford, Margot, 71. Harvey, Philip, 19 (BOTTOM). Hunter Douglas, 133 (BOTTOM). Hurni, Jean-Claude, 26 (ALL), 39 (ALL), 41 (TOP RIGHT AND BOTTOM). Jado Bathroom and Hardware Manufacturing Corp., 97 (BOTTOM LEFT). JELD-WEN, Inc., 131. Kohler Co., 62 (ALL), 63 (RIGHT), 79 (TOP LEFT), 80 (BOTTOM LEFT), 83 (BOTTOM), 84 (TOP), 85 (BOTTOM), 91 (TOP TWO), 93 (TOP AND MIDDLE), 95 (BOTTOM LEFT), 96, 97 (TOP RIGHT), 98 (TOP), 99 (TOP LEFT AND BOTTOM TWO), 113 (ALL), 135, 143, 148, 154. Kohler Ann Sacks, 103 (TOP RIGHT). Kohler Kallista, 81 (TOP), 86 (TOP AND BOTTOM LEFT), 114 (RIGHT TOP). Kohler Robern, 111 (TOP LEFT), 114 (ALL EXCEPT RIGHT TOP), 125. Kohler Sterling, 79 (TOP RIGHT AND BOTTOM FAR RIGHT). Krukowski, Dennis, 18, 22, 30, 32 (LEFT), 48, 58, 69. LASCO Bathware, 80 (MIDDLE AND BOTTOM RIGHT). Laufen International, 119. Livingston, David Duncan, 2, 9, 13, 14, 15 (ALL), 20, 21 (TOP RIGHT), 24, 25 (TOP LEFT AND BOTTOM), 28, 29, 31 (TOP RIGHT AND BOTTOM), 32 (RIGHT), 35 (TOP), 41 (TOP LEFT), 50 (TOP AND BOTTOM LEFT), 53, 55, 57 (TOP RIGHT), 59, 60 (TOP AND BOTTOM LEFT), 66 (BOTTOM LEFT), 67 (ALL), 70 (TOP LEFT; BOTTOM LEFT AND BOTTOM RIGHT), 72, 74, 75 (TOP LEFT). 186. MasterBrand Cabinets, Inc., 105 (TOP). McGrath, Norman, 165. Moen, Inc., 97 (BOTTOM RIGHT), 110 (LEFT). O'Hagen, John/SPC photo collection, 40. O'Hara, Stephen, for Hometips, 157, 158 (ALL EXCEPT BOTTOM), 159 (TOP), 160 (FAR TOP RIGHT; SECOND FROM BOTTOM AND BOTTOM), 163 (BOTTOM). Olympic Paints and Stains, 123. Pella Corp., 128 (RIGHT), 129 (ALL). Plate, Norman A., 159 (THIRD FROM TOP). Price Pfister, Inc., 97 (TOP LEFT), 98 (MIDDLE), 212. RSI Home Products, 105 (BOTTOM), 107 (ALL). Rutherford, Mark, 159 (SECOND FROM BOTTOM), 188 (ALL), 189 (ALL EXCEPT TOP AND BOTTOM RIGHT), 190 (ALL), 191 (BOTTOM LEFT AND BOTTOM RIGHT). Skott, Michael, 47, 49 (TOP LEFT). Speakman Co., 88 (TOP THREE). Springs Window Fashions LP, 132 (LEFT), 133 (TOP). Street-Porter, Tim, 19 (TOP), 36 (ALL), 49 (BOTTOM), 51, 54 (TOP), 57 (BOTTOM). Thomas Lighting, (ALL EXCEPT MIDDLE LEFT). Valspar Corp., 122. Vanden Brink, Brian, 8, 23, 33, 34, 35 (BOTTOM), 52, 61, 63 (LEFT), 65, 70 (TOP LEFT). Vandervort, Don, 10, 136, 144, 149, 150 (ALL), 151 (ALL), 152, 153 (ALL), 155 (ALL), 161 (ALL). VELUX America Inc., 77 (TOP), 128 (LEFT), 130 (ALL). Vendetta, Christopher, for Hometips, 163 (RIGHT BOTTOM AND SECOND FROM BOTTOM), 170–173 (ALL), 175 (ALL), 176–185 (ALL), 189 (TOP TWO AND BOTTOM RIGHT), 191 (TOP LEFT AND TOP RIGHT), 192–195 (ALL), 197 (MIDDLE; SECOND FROM BOTTOM AND BOTTOM), 208–211 (ALL), 216–219 (ALL). Wakely, David, 12, 16, 17, 25 (TOP RIGHT), 31 (TOP LEFT), 49 (TOP RIGHT), 57 (TOP LEFT), 64, 66 (TOP), 75 (RIGHT). Waterpik Technologies, 88 (BOTTOM). Waverly Home Classics, 124 (ALL). Zenith Products Corp., 106 (LEFT THREE), 108 (ALL), 109 (ALL), 115 (TOP FIVE). Zepeda, Eric, 38 (LEFT).

index

index

index